Wreck Hunter

The Quest
for
Lost Shipwrecks

Terry Dwyer

Pottersfield Press, Lawrencetown Beach, Nova Scotia, Canada

Library and Archives Canada Cataloguing in Publication

Dwyer, Terry

Wreck hunter : the quest for lost shipwrecks / Terry Dwyer.

ISBN 1-895900-67-0

1. Deep diving. 2. Shipwrecks – Nova Scotia. 3. Underwater
archaeology – Nova Scotia. 4. Dwyer, Terry. 5. Divers – Canada – Biography.
I. Title.

FC2320.S5D99 2004 627'.72'09716   C2004-904688-8

Cover photo: by Alan Aitken

Cover design: by Larry Burke

Pottersfield Press acknowledges the ongoing support of The Canada Council for the Arts, as well as the Nova Scotia Department of Tourism, Culture and Heritage, Cultural Affairs Division. We also acknowledge the financial support of the Government of Canada through the Book Publishing Industry Development Program for our publishing activities.

Pottersfield Press
83 Leslie Road
East Lawrencetown
Nova Scotia, Canada, B2Z 1P8
Website: www.pottersfieldpress.com
To order, phone 1-800-NIMBUS9 (1-800-646-2879)
Printed in Canada

Nothing in the world can take the place of persistence. Talent will not; nothing is more common than unsuccessful men with talent. Genius will not; unrewarded genius is almost a proverb. Education will not; the world is full of educated derelicts. Persistence and determination alone are omnipotent.

– Calvin Coolidge

Table of Contents

Dedication		7
Acknowledgments		9
Foreword by Alex Storm		11
Preface		13
1	An Introduction to the Shipwrecks of Nova Scotia	21
2	Cape Breton Island	23
3	St. Paul Island: The Graveyard of the Gulf	36
4	Scatarie Island	62
5	Louisbourg Harbour	72
6	Halifax Harbour and Approaches	83
7	Cape Sable and Seal Island	105
8	Pirates and Privateers in Nova Scotia	120
9	In Search of Shipwrecks and Treasure	126
10	Discoveries in Waiting	137
11	Wreck Hunting Tools and Techniques	144
12	Scuba Tourism Opportunities	158
13	Scuba Diving: The Ultimate Adventure	162
14	Boat Diving in Nova Scotia	167
15	Aids to Navigation	175
16	Underwater Video	179
17	Deep Star Exploration	185
18	The Adventure Continues	188
19	Some Final Thoughts	191
The Responsible Diver Program		195
Recommended Websites		197
Selected Bibliography		200
About the Author		207

Dedication

To my wife and soulmate Suzie and to our newborn daughter Holly Marie, you both continue to inspire me and you will always be the most important part of my life. On past adventures, I have discovered virgin shipwrecks off the coast of St. Paul Island and I have experienced the sheer excitement of swimming alongside a sixteen foot beluga whale named Wilma in Guysborough, Nova Scotia, but it all pales in comparison to the excitement, happiness and joy that you both bring into my life. I love you both very much, you are my true treasures.

This book is also dedicated to my mother Cecilia Irene Dwyer, to Mary Mombourquette, and to my very good friends and associates Bernie McIassac, Rob Mack, Jim Johnson, and David Dow who all passed away before it was finished. Thank you once again for believing in me and for the many years of kindness, constant encouragement and unwavering support. Without it, none of what is written in this book would have been accomplished or even dreamed of. You always believed in, but never lived to see, the realization of my dreams. The world is a much better place for all of you having walked through it.

To my dad Tommy, my brothers Danny and Timmy, and my sisters Tracey and Tammy, thank you; we had a great child-hood and upbringing. I often think about my childhood years and especially the good times we all shared growing up in New Waterford, Cape Breton.

This book is also dedicated to my friends, associates and the many divers who for years have been generous with their time, continue to take the risks and absorb the financial costs that are associated with searching for lost shipwrecks. These everyday people from all walks of life are a very large part of this book, and I would like to sincerely say thank you for more than twenty years of great adventures and hundreds of exciting dives.

Acknowledgments

This book would never have been written without the able assistance of many individuals who unselfishly shared their personal time and information so that others may experience the adventure of searching for lost shipwrecks. It is my sincerest hope that I have not forgotten to thank any of the people, friends and associates who made this book possible.

Many thanks to Steve Crain, James Semple, Albert Coffill, Bill Woludka, Albert Leahy, Steve and Cathy Tower, Gary Spears, Kevin Gates, Chris Deviller, Hardy Kalberlah, Gair White, Joe Christie, Doug and Dora Symonds, John Symonds, Donnie Mahannie, Paul Fitzgerald, Johnny Fitzgerald, Troy Fitzgerald, Billy Budge, Jack and Lizzie Bird, Melissa Marlowe, Doug Hrvoic, Dean and Paulette Bailey, Ross Hammond, Cal and Glenys Fleming, Heather Ward, Dave Clancy, Palmer Sargent, Philippe Beaudry, Harvey Leroy, Don Young, Len Hart, Gordon McVicar, George K. O'Neil, Keith Woodill, Brian MacDonald, Jimmy and Kim Taylor, Kevin Nickelson, Joe Westhaver, Willis Stevens, Jim Ringer, Scott Carpenter, George Guthro, Gilles Paquet, and Vern Gordon and John Chidley.

A special thank you to Archie Rose, Ed Barrington and Alex Storm, my mentors and the undisputed three wise men of shipwrecks, salvage and treasure. Thank you for your continued assistance, patience, guidance, inspiration, friendship, and support.

A very special thank you to Sam and Jennifer Millett, Gabe and Maria Carrier, Scott and Kim Fitzgerald, Robert Marx, Hubert Hall, Kelly Fitzgerald, E.R. Lynmire, Glen and Tanya Burnett, Bob Smith, Harry Dort, Jane Everitt, Norbert Duckworth, Colin Millar, Jim Eddington, Robert Guertin, Randy Brooks, Dianne Barrington, John Schumacher, Jimmy Mullins, Bob Anthony, Gordon Fader, Bob O Miller, David and Diana Burnett, Trevor Bast, Loren Johnson, John Theobald, Derek King, Liz Rolf, Dave and Susan Millhouser, Harvey and Ann Morash, Glenda Dugas, Mark Stanton, Ron Hand, Ken Moore, Rudi Asseer, John Mills, George Hickey, Ned Middleton, Walter and Donna Petrie, John Oldham, Dave Barron, Alan Aitken for the cover photo, Larry Burke for the cover design, Chuck and Carol MacMillan, David Gough, Fred Wade, Ron Laing, Doug Carmichael, Todd Murchie, Blair Christian, Ally Wynn, George Brooks, Phil Nuytten, Simon Morris, Doug Pemberton, Mike and Lori Covert, Sam Warwick, Mick "Mad Dog" Cullen, Phil Waddington, Robin Adams, Ron Blundon, Paul Smood, Helen and Howard Carby, John Pierre, Mike Wamboldt, Debbie Johnson, Dana Johnson, and Carol Johnson. Ben Jamin, Mark Rowsome, Ron Newcombe, Doug Shand, Rick and Debbie Stanley, Gerard Chidley, Herbo Humphreys Jr., Tim Hudson and Ben "Mongo" Marich.

Foreword

With Nova Scotia shipwreck diving on the increase, Terry Dwyer has already made many contributions to further scuba tourism, recreational diving and undersea exploration. He can now add this book to his achievements. This book is not merely written by an academic, but by a diver who has "lived the life"! Indeed, the diving community is fortunate to have an enthusiast like Terry in their midst. A tenacious researcher, he diligently pursues elusive bits of historical evidence with the same determination demonstrated in all of his endeavours. Written with great enthusiasm and clarity, this informative book makes an interesting wreck dive much more so, by making the exciting background stories available. His love of underwater exploration shines through in this very readable book.

Alex Storm
Author, historian and
retired wreck hunter
Seaweed and Gold
Canada's Treasure Hunt

Preface

I was born and raised in the coastal community of New Water-ford, Nova Scotia, a coal-mining town located on the Atlantic Ocean. As far back as I can remember I have always been fascinated with scuba diving and sunken ships. As a teenager I watched the *Undersea World of Jacques Cousteau* television specials and was captivated and mesmerized by the images.

At fourteen years old I was determined to become a scuba diver. I spent the entire winter of 1977 shoveling driveways, picking and selling bootleg coal from the Lingan Coal Mine, painting houses, cutting and splitting hardwood in my parents' driveway then delivering it in half-ton truck loads throughout the New Waterford area to save $600 to pay for a scuba course. I learned very early in life the value of initiative, tenacity and plain, old-fashioned hard work. Somewhere in that process I was bitten by the entrepreneur bug. In the summer of 1978 I was a fifteen-year-old grade nine student at Breton Education Centre in New Waterford when I finally earned my Open Water Diver Certification at Aqua Dive Scuba Shop in Sydney. My first open water dive took place near the Gabarus lighthouse.

For my grade ten law class I did a report on treasure hunting and salvage laws. As part of the project I telephoned Alex Storm in Louisbourg several times and asked him if he would agree to be interviewed. He reluctantly consented and, as a result, I got to spend an evening talking to Alex Storm about his personal treasure hunting experiences. I brought along a tape recorder and a sixty-minute cassette, which I still have today. The interview lasted several hours and that particular night sparked a passionate interest in shipwrecks that would change my life forever.

I discovered my first shipwreck during the summer of 1979 while diving with David Odo, a cousin of mine from New Waterford. We were exploring a cove at the foot of Park Street in the town of Dominion, near Glace Bay. At the entrance to the cove in twenty feet of water I came across what resembled three-foot-long, dull yellowish-greenish L-shaped tire irons sticking up from the sea bed. I had a vision of tomorrow's newspaper headline: *Local village boy makes big discovery*. I recovered one of the odd-looking "tire irons" and brought it ashore. The very next day I was at Alex Storm's residence in Louisbourg showing him my find and asking him if he could identify it. My L-shaped tire iron turned out to be a bronze spike, probably from a nineteenth-century sailing ship.

I spent the rest of the year clearing propellers for fishermen after school and on weekends. This source of newfound income inspired me to start my own business – Sea Divers, which allowed me to buy more scuba gear. I soon found myself the only sixteen-year-old grade ten student with my own car and disposable income. Shortly thereafter I decided that school was not for me. I wanted to become an entrepreneur and to make my living as a professional diver. I looked up Off Shore Diving and Salvage in the telephone book, phoned them and asked if they were hiring. The gentleman on the other end of the phone asked who I was and if I had any experience in commercial diving. I explained that I had been clearing propellers for fishermen after school and on weekends. I had no real experience but I wanted to become a commercial diver and was willing to start at the bottom (pardon the pun) and work my way up, learning the game. He politely told me that there was nothing available right now and suggested I look at attending a commercial diving school or perhaps look elsewhere to get some experience.

My tenacious personality took over and resulted in regular weekly telephone calls to Off Shore Diving and Salvage, and it didn't stop there. I soon located their office at the residence of Ed Barrington in Sydney, so I thought why not drop by and introduce myself. Still no work available. I stepped up the visits and even threw in a Christmas card. I stopped short of pitching a tent on his lawn, as I felt I was becoming a bit of a nuisance (I believe today the proper word is stalker). So, in a last ditch effort, I once again telephoned Ed Barrington and told him I would work for free for the entire summer if he would hire me. He paused and thought for a minute, then spoke the words, "You're hired. Start Monday morning."

Off Shore Diving and Salvage had been awarded the contract to cut up and remove some old shipwrecks behind what was then the Isle Royal Hotel in Sydney Harbour. I showed up Monday morning (a half hour early) and was informed I would be paid $5.50 per hour and would work as a general labourer or, as it was unofficially called, a "grunt." The job would last a few months then I would be laid off, which is how the commercial diving business works. Although I didn't do any actual diving, I did get to observe and sometimes help the divers with their equipment.

In the spring of 1979 I read an ad in the *Cape Breton Post* looking for divers. It turned out to be a local treasure hunting company called Man 4 Research and Development, which was owned and operated by Joe Starr, Robert MacKinnon and Jimmy Mullins. They were accepting résumés for the upcoming season. I sent in a detailed résumé; less than a week later I started work full time as a general labourer and deck hand (are you seeing a pattern here?) and I was to be paid $125 for a 40-hour workweek. While I got to do very little diving, I did learn a lot about doing research and about the treasure hunting business. For five years I worked out of their base of operations at Myra Gut, Cape Breton. From 1985 to the present I found steady employment in Halifax in the commercial, scientific and recreational scuba industry.

In 1992, Jim Eddington and I started our own diving company – Deep Star Resources. It would be the beginning of a great adventure that would last years. From the very beginning Deep Star built its reputation on underwater video and photography.

We specialized in scientific diving and shipwreck surveys, and we pioneered scuba tourism development. We also dabbled in the off-shore geophysical business with an old side scan sonar system and marine magnetometer that we purchased at a government surplus Crown Assets auction.

In September of 1995, Lightstorm Entertainment out of Hollywood, California, selected Deep Star to assist in logistics, diving support services and location scouting for part of a feature film in production, entitled *Planet Ice*. We would find out later that *Planet Ice* was the working title for the film *Titanic*. Using leased Russian MIR submarines and state-of-the-art underwater lighting equipment, one of Canada's most successful movie directors, James Cameron, and Hollywood cinematographer Al Giddings were setting out to capture the best film images ever taken of the *Titanic*.

Halifax was chosen as the base of operations for the 460-foot Russian support vessel RV *Akademik Keldysh* to conduct a top-secret expedition to film the remains of *Titanic* in August of 1995. The underwater site chosen for the various tests and work-ups with the two Russian subs – *MIR 1* and *MIR 2* – and the lighting towers that were eventually used to light the *Titanic* for the film was about six miles outside of Lunenburg, Nova Scotia. Deep Star supplied three camera assistants/safety divers and considerable rental equipment, ranging from a Zodiac inflatable to ten sets of scuba gear.

I was part of a team that, to simulate realistic conditions, worked in sixty feet of water at night, adjusting, testing and recovering the light towers. On our first shift we worked in shallow water for twenty-four hours, straight through the night and well into the next day. I can't convey to you the level of excitement and the rush of adrenaline we all experienced working on this project. Lightstorm Entertainment also rented Deep Star's VX-3 Hi-8 camera as a back-up system for Al Giddings to use, and it was carried onboard the *MIR 1* as it surveyed the *Titanic* on more than thirty dives.

Lightstorm Entertainment contracted us again in July of 1996 to assist them in scouting possible locations outside of Halifax Harbour. As well, we carried out more underwater lighting tests, again at night but this time our location was twenty-eight miles

Movie Marine Canada divemaster Blair Christian, actor Kevin Spacey, and Movie Marine Canada scuba instructor to the stars Sam Millett on the set of *The Shipping News* in Halifax. Sam Millett trained Kevin Spacey to scuba dive and was his personal safety diver during the water scenes in the movie.
(Photo by Robert Guertin, Communication Concepts)

outside of Halifax Harbour. During this project I conceived the idea to create Movie Marine Canada to provide diving support services for the film, video and motion picture industry. At this time I met Vince Pace, the owner/operator of Pace Technologies. Pace designed and built the underwater lights used in the motion picture *Titanic*.

After the project wrapped up production, I telephoned Vince Pace in Los Angeles, California, and asked if we could represent his company here in Atlantic Canada. Vince was reluctant as we had very little knowledge of or experience with high-powered, sophisticated underwater lighting systems. I made a counter suggestion; I and two associates (Todd Murchie and Doug Carmichael) would fly to L.A. for a week and cover all our own expenses if Vince agreed to train us as technicians on Pace lighting systems. He did and Movie Marine Canada was born. Since then we have been contracted to supply the diving support services on just about every major motion picture filmed in Halifax that involved working on or around the water.

Another Movie Marine Canada divemaster, Ally Wynn, on her way to work on the set of *K-19 The Widow Maker*. (Photo by Terry Dwyer)

In the movie industry you're only as good as the last project you worked on. Movie Marine Canada has always been invited back. Most recently, we supplied the diving support services for the major motion pictures *K-19 The Widow Maker*, *The Shipping News*, *Deeply*, and *The Weight of Water*, parts of which were filmed here in Nova Scotia. We also supplied the diving support services for the TV movies *Shattered City: The Halifax Explosion*, *Blessed Stranger: The Aftermath of Swiss Air Flight 111*, and for the Discovery Channel TV series *High Seas Rescue* and *Oceans of Mystery*.

Over the past eight years we have worked on various movie sets as safety divers for some of Hollywood's biggest stars, including Harrison Ford, Liam Neeson, Elizabeth Hurley, Sean Penn, Kirstin Dunst, Sara Polley, and Kevin Spacey (whom we trained to scuba dive in preparation for his water scenes in *The Shipping News*).

Over the years, I've had the privilege to have worked on and been involved in some very exciting and fascinating projects, ranging from surveying sunken shipwrecks to organizing the first ever international expedition to St. Paul Island. I have also had the privilege to work with and dive with some very fine people. Some of these exciting projects and fascinating people are described and mentioned in this book, but there are many others that will have to wait for volume two. The idea to write a book and to include some of the projects and adventures that I have been involved in over the years was suggested to me time and time again by many of my friends and associates who work in this business. It has taken me many years to finally get around to doing it, and it has brought back a lot of great memories.

But enough about me; let's get back to why I wrote this book. Over the last twenty years, I got one hell of an education in scuba diving and in shipwrecks – how to research and how to find them – and I learned a great deal about the business of shipwreck exploration. The point I want to make is that anybody can find shipwrecks.

The information presented in this book has come from many sources, including archives, libraries, personal conversations with retired treasure hunters and salvage divers, various communications, letters, correspondence, old and rare books, and reports and documents that I have obtained over the years and are now part of my personal collection. Where possible I have included references as to where the information originated.

I have been collecting and gathering research on specific shipwrecks here in Nova Scotia that are, in my opinion, valuable and well worth searching for. I have spent thousands of hours and as many dollars gathering this information. It has been a labour of love that has taken me twenty-five years to compile and it still continues today. In some cases, I have exact references; in other cases all I have are names, dates and rough areas. Any type of shipwreck research is very time consuming, always ongoing and at times can be costly. It can also be as simple and as inexpensive as writing a letter to London, England.

I encourage the reader to take the time to visit the local library and the various institutes and archives that house a tremendous collection of research material on shipwrecks. I have also included a bibliography at the back of the book to assist any would-be wreck hunters. In Nova Scotia you might be surprised at what you can ferret out in terms of interesting and historically accurate information.

For the diver or would-be explorer who is interested enough and does his or her own research, there are volumes of books, old newspapers, documents, records and information just waiting to be sifted through. With some effort, some detective work, a little patience and time you too can bring the history of a lost shipwreck back to life and hopefully begin your own personal adventure in or out of the water.

Terry Dwyer
Halifax, Nova Scotia
November 2004

1

An Introduction to the Shipwrecks of Nova Scotia

There are shipwrecks in every part of the world. In Nova Scotia they can usually be found in areas along the coastline that are rich in history and shipping traffic. The province of Nova Scotia is 360 miles long and has nearly 4,700 miles of coastline. There is no part of the province that is more than forty miles from the sea. Nova Scotia was, and still is, connected to the shipping lanes of countries all over the world, and there is more than five hundred years of history to research and read about.

With a nautical history dating back hundreds of years, Nova Scotia boasts one of the world's greatest concentrations of shipwrecks. Today many historians and professional researchers conservatively estimate that there are in excess of ten thousand shipwrecks off the coast of Nova Scotia. There are many reasons why this is so. Shipwrecks can be caused by a number of things, primarily bad weather conditions such as fog, high winds and storms at sea. In the winter, blowing snow and freezing rain take their toll on ships. Two world wars were responsible for sinking hundreds of ships off our coast and killing thousands of men and women who sailed on them.

Foreign captains unfamiliar with our waters quite often paid the price with their ships. Nova Scotia has a short summer season and many unpredictable weather patterns. There are also hundreds of islands, shoals, reefs, and partially submerged rocks that dot our coastline from Sydney to Yarmouth.

Nova Scotia is very rich in history and the thousands of shipwrecks that still exist today are very much a part of that history. Even more staggering is the fact that only five percent of these ten thousand known shipwrecks have ever been located, visited or documented by divers.

As a scuba diver, when I encounter a shipwreck for the first time, I experience a sensation of mystery. Any diver who has had the opportunity to visit a shipwreck can appreciate the mystery that surrounds it. It doesn't matter if the wreck is resting on the bottom relatively intact, or whether it resembles an underwater junkyard of twisted metal that has no recognizable definition or shape to it. Regardless of its condition, every shipwreck has an interesting history. The story of how and why it came to rest on our Nova Scotia shores will live in your mind's eye every time you visit it.

As you begin to explore a shipwreck over a period of several dives, you will soon be able to distinguish the bow section, the mid section and the stern section of the wreck – providing the wreck is not scattered over a large area or broken in two. In some cases, the wreck or parts of it have been salvaged over the years. Sometimes, especially here on the rugged east coast, the forces of Mother Nature combined with the tremendous and relentless power of the ocean can completely disintegrate a shipwreck over time and little or no trace of a wreck can be found. Even icebergs can destroy a shipwreck in a matter of a few years. Either way, what you experience on your first wreck dive is the beginning of an exciting and continuing lifelong adventure.

2

Cape Breton Island

Cape Breton Island is located at the extreme northeast end of Nova Scotia on the rocky coast of eastern Canada. The island is 110 miles in length and roughly 87 miles across at its widest point. The whole of the island, with the exception of the northwest coast, is indented by deep bays and inlets often terminating in excellent harbours. The summer months from June to September provide the best window of opportunity for scuba diving and searching for shipwrecks.

It was on the morning of June 24, 1497, that John Cabot and his son Sebastian landed on the beach in the shadow of Sugar Loaf Mountain in Aspy Bay and called the island *"prima terra vista."* There is evidence that the Portuguese explorer João Alvares Fagundes arrived about 1520 and attempted to settle Ingonish and St. Ann's Bay. However, old records recently unearthed in Spain now show that the Basques actually crossed the Atlantic Ocean even earlier in pursuit of whales and discovered the lucrative fishing grounds of the Grand Banks. It is believed that they also discovered and named the island of Cape Breton. They even penetrated the Gulf of St. Lawrence before Columbus reached America.

But the history of Cape Breton goes back much further than that. In fact, over the last nine hundred years (that we know about at this time) there were other inhabitants that included the Maritime Archaic Indians, the Mi'kmaq, the Vikings and possibly others. According to certain ancient Icelandic manuscripts, or sagas, the whole of the eastern coast of America from Greenland to Nantucket was discovered by Norweigan rovers in the tenth century, soon after the settlement of Iceland and Greenland. It's stated in the sagas that frequent voyages were made during the eleventh and twelfth centuries to various parts of the newfound lands. There is a great deal of research that records English, French, Spanish and Portugese ships exploring, and even attempting to settle, parts of Cape Breton Island throughout the fifteenth, sixteenth and seventeenth centuries. Some even wrecked here. With a history dating back over one thousand years, Cape Breton Island is one of the oldest and most historic parts of Canada and historians speculate there may be in excess of one thousand ships wrecked along Cape Breton Island alone.

One of the earliest recorded shipwrecks (that we know of at this time) to occur on Cape Breton Island was the seventy-ton English warship *Chancewell*, which wrecked on June 23, 1597. Historians and scholars have narrowed the suspected site of this wreck down to two possible areas: St. Ann's Bay or possibly near Ingonish. To date it has never been found and while not a treasure ship, its historical significance is of paramount importance as it is the oldest known shipwreck to have occurred on Cape Breton Island.

Cape North and Aspy Bay

Cape North lies at the northeastern extremity of Cape Breton Island and rises abruptly as a rocky headland to a height of 1,100 feet. It has no shallow water at its base, but around to the eastward at Money Point a few rocks show themselves. To the Mi'kmaq Cape North was *Uktutunook* or "highest mountain." Other versions like Cap du Nord and Cape North are simply descriptive names given to that area, and the beauty of the landscape cannot be overstated.

Similarly, Aspy Bay was known as *Wegwaak* or "turning suddenly." The French knew the area as Havre d'Aspe or D'Achepe, which may have been patterned after the Mi'kmaq word for codfish, *apaqo* or *apago*. To the Basques who fished in these waters, it was Pic d'Aspe after the Pyrenean mountain of the same name. Regardless of its origins it is easy to see how the English arrived at the name Aspy Bay, although the origin of their other name for the region, Egmont Bay, is unknown.

To mariners, it can be particularly treacherous and in addition to the topography, a peculiar phenomenon at Aspy Bay gave early sailors an extra reason for caution. The bay is more than eight miles across and four miles long. Along its shores, Atlantic storms have swept a mass of fine sand, which forms a beautiful beach. At places this sand is of a black colour, very heavy, with a metallic lustre, and looks like granulated iron. It is probably on this account that compasses will not work properly at any part of this bay, in consequence of which if proper notice be not taken, much property may be lost. In the month of September 1882, two large steamships took shelter in the bay during a stormy night, and in the morning, the captain and one of the crew came ashore, seeking assistance, assuring the people that his compass was of no service to him.

Nestled in the heart of Aspy Bay is the coastal fishing community of Dingwall. One of several settlements on the bay, its name originates from Scotland, which was the supposed birthplace of the much-maligned King Macbeth. Norse in origin, the name Dingwall comes from *ting* (parliament) and *voir* (valley). From there, a thousand years ago, the Vikings governed the north. These Vikings also crossed the Atlantic and roamed the shores at the top of Cape Breton Island. They got word back to Europe by way of the Norse sagas, which spoke of Vinland and Markland. About eight hundred years later Scottish settlers came to these shores.

On maps from the early 1800s it was known as Young's Cove. Among the first settlers and grantees for land was Walter Young in 1827. In the late 1870s Robert Dingwall, who kept a small general store there, made an application for a post office, and suggested to the government that the place be named Dingwall. By provincial statute in 1883, the name of Young's Cove was changed to Dingwall. Today fishing and tourism are the main industries. Dingwall is also where one of the richest shipwrecks in this hemisphere occurred: the *Auguste* wrecked in a violent winter storm back in November of 1761.

The Wreck of the Auguste

The winds of war carried defeat to the French army in 1759 at the Plains of Abraham. When the British took Montreal from the French in 1760, the flag of the Golden Lilies was pulled down for the last time and the Union Jack flew over every fort and garrison in North America. The new British possession was no place for any loyal Frenchman. As soon as the articles of capitulation were signed, the British began to send their prisoners back to France. But transport was scarce and the work of evacuation was necessarily slow. A year after capitulation there were still French soldiers remaining in New France.

In the autumn of 1761, on September 27, one year after the surrender of Montreal, Governor James Murray, a fiery Scottish aristocrat, received a number of French officials, aristocrats, artisans, wealthy merchants, high ranking military officers, soldiers and civilians, rank and file, great and small, at Castle St. Louis. He made ready for their exile the fully rigged ship *Auguste*, under the command of an English master, Captain Joseph Knowles, and placed them all onboard.

The *Auguste* was a merchant transport of no particular fame or consequence; she was French built and spent at least part of her career as a merchant vessel, carrying sugar, coffee and cotton in the Caribbean. The British captured her on August 18, 1756. At the time, she had a crew of 39 men and mounted just six cannons, but was equipped to carry as many as 16 guns. The *Auguste* was sold by the navy as a prize and the new British owners used her as a merchant ship.

The *Auguste* arrived in Quebec on July 22, 1761, carrying a wide array of goods. Once the cargo was unloaded, Governor

Murray commandeered the *Auguste* to accommodate the overflow of the Canadian exiles and their families from two other ships, the *Jane* and the *Molineux*. The *Auguste* was described in the harbour records as a 245-ton ship, with nine guns, foreign built but registered in London. She was three-masted with square sails, and although the tonnage was known the actual dimensions remain a mystery.

One particular prisoner, Luc de La Corne, was placed on the *Auguste*. He was no ordinary man; a seasoned merchant, soldier and fur trader, his family name is written large in the annals of New France and Acadia. He came from an influential and wealthy family with a military background, his father being town-major of the garrison at Quebec.

La Corne's brother, Louis, was known as the Chevalier de La Corne because he was the eldest son. Louis, aged fifty-eight, had been a captain since 1744 and a Knight of the Order of St. Louis since 1749 for his actions against Colonel Arthur Noble and the British at Grand Pré in 1747. An explorer and a fur trader, he was among the very first white men to penetrate the perilous interior of the continent and to see the limitless prairies alive with moving seas of buffalo. He had established a wide chain of trading posts across Canada. He was commandant of the western fur trading posts, travelling as far west as the forks of the North and South Saskatchewan Rivers where he built Fort La Corne.

Luc de La Corne had been a man or war from his youth and had won the coveted Cross of St. Louis in 1759 for the successful ambush of a British supply column, during which he destroyed the supplies, captured sixty-four prisoners and took eighty scalps. A renowned partisan leader, adept in Indian warfare, Luc could speak several languages from Sioux to Mi'kmaq and was chief interpreter for the government. He had shared in the great victory of Montcalm over Abercromby at Carillon (Ticonderoga, New York), and had watched Amherst's flotilla bearing ten thousand men shoot the rapids on their victorious way to Montreal. He had served with distinction and had been twice wounded, and now with two of his sons, his brother Louis and two nephews, he was on his way to France. By the time of his deportation Luc de La Corne was one of the richest men in Canada.

The Order of St. Louis cross recovered from the *Auguste* site in 1977. King Louis XIV of France created the order in 1693, which was reserved for officers who had distinguished themselves in battle. The badge was a gold and silver Maltese cross, with fleurs-de-lys between the arms, a medallion showed Louis on one side, and an upright sword through a laurel wreath on the other. The motto was *bellicae virtutis praemium*, the reward of warring valour. (Photo by John Schumacher)

Fifty-year-old Luc wasn't happy about the mode of transport. He actually offered to buy a more suitable vessel, but he was forced to settle for the *Auguste*. Looking around the ship, La Corne would have found himself among very familiar faces. Most of the male passengers were members of the Canadian Colonial Force, which had been formed in 1683. Fourteen Canadian officers and their families were aboard, all prominent and well-connected men, figures of influence and authority. Seven of the wealthiest women in Canada were also onboard, along with many other very distinguished Frenchmen. Fifteen officers and men made up the crew, with 106 passengers together with all their personal wealth and belongings. In all there were 121 people aboard the *Auguste*, including women and children.

The *Auguste* sailed on October 15, 1761, under a white flag and with one gun for signaling purposes. The only charts onboard were of the French coast, and there was no pilot to see her through the dangerous shoals at the mouth of the lower St. Lawrence. La Corne promptly bought, for $500 Spanish, the use of the captain's cabin. La Corne kept a diary that gives a vivid record of the ill-fated voyage. The voyage was a disaster: the ship's galley caught fire; she narrowly missed being wrecked several times and on November 15, 1761, she was finally blown ashore near Dingwall Harbour, at the mouth of Middle Pond in Aspy Bay, Cape Breton.

There were only seven survivors, including Luc de La Corne, out of 121 people and they suffered dreadful privations. Setting out for help, they were eventually rescued by Mi'kmaq who helped some of them get to Quebec. Many of the drowned women washed up on an area of the beach known locally for some time as Ladies Beach. The wreck of the *Auguste* was forgotten and faded into history for the next 216 years.

Then in the summer of 1977, Sydney-based Offshore Diving and Salvage had their dive vessel, *Offshore Salvor*, tied up in Dingwall Harbour waiting for the weather to change so they could steam to St. Paul Island to carry out salvage operations on known wrecks. While in Dingwall, they decided to search for any signs of the *Auguste*. Within hours divers John Schumacher and Robert Anthony located an anchor chain, then an anchor and a cannon. The cannon and cannon balls soon gave way to silver coins.

Offshore Diving and Salvage reported their find to the Receiver of Wrecks in Sydney, then to the federal Department of Indian and Northern Affairs. They soon found themselves in a joint venture with Parks Canada Underwater Marine Archaeology Unit. During the 1977-78 field season, coins of various descriptions were discovered. These coins represented approximately 31 percent (1,242) of the total number of artifacts recovered. All the coins retrieved from the site were of the milled (machine-struck) variety and all date between 1677 and 1759.

The most notable artifact ever recovered was a gold cross called the Order of St. Louis. The second such cross ever recovered from a shipwreck in Canada. (The first was recovered by Alex Storm on the *Le Chameau* wreck site on May 20, 1968.) It was a spectacular find discovered by Offshore Diving and Salvage diver John Schumacher. That cross is believed to have belonged to either Louis the Chevalier de La Corne or his younger brother Luc.

Twenty years later in 2001 an American-Canadian consortium, the Auguste Expedition Company, started to rework the original site. Their most notable find was during the summer of 2003 when diver Paul Fitzgerald of Dingwall found yet another Order of St. Louis cross. In 2003, John Schumacher filed an application for a treasure trove license encompassing an area extending out eight square miles on all sides around the outside perimeter of the original 1977-78 site. He was eventually granted the license in May 2004, setting the stage for a new chapter that has yet to be written on the search for the *Auguste* treasure.

Luc de La Corne died in 1784 at the age of 73 at his home in Montreal. Almost 250 years later the *Auguste* treasure, consisting of vast amounts of jewelry, gold and silver coins estimated to be worth millions of dollars, has still not been found. To date no one has located the actual stern section of the *Auguste*, which is believed to have contained the majority of the valuables on board. Somewhere resting on the seabed off the coast of Dingwall in Aspy Bay, a lost fortune is still waiting to be discovered.

The Wreck of the Ariadne

Just a few miles south of Aspy Bay is the coastal fishing community of Neil's Harbour. This area has a great many shipwrecks as well, the most notable called the *Ariadne*. On the night of October 7, 1896, in the midst of a violent gale, the Anglican rector of Neil's Harbour, the Rev. Robert Atkinson-Smith, spotted a large piece of driftwood from a recent wreck floating on the waves. The priest dressed quickly in oil skins and hip boots and organized a search party to locate the vessel and, if possible, rescue some of her crew. After thirty-six hours in a storm-tossed dory, Atkinson-Smith and the two fishermen who accompanied him discovered the Norwegian barque *Ariadne* wrecked off MacKinnon's Point at Green Cove. They rescued two crewmen, recovered three bodies and returned to Neil's Harbour.

The parish record book records, "Bark *Ariadne* of Crishana, Captain Paulsen, from Greenock, Scotland, for Bay Verte, New Brunswick, foundered at North Bay, Ingonish, Cape Breton, on October 7, 1896. Ten lives lost." New Haven fishermen helped the men of Neil's Harbour with the unhappy task of building coffins and one of the local merchants donated the cloth to cover

The communion set presented in 1897 by the Vice Consul of Norway to the Rev. Robert Atkinson-Smith of Neil's Harbour for rescuing Norweigian sailors. It is still used today. (Photo by Terry Dwyer)

the caskets. Green spruce boughs were placed on the lid of each coffin in the form of a cross, and the whole village joined the two survivors at the funeral of their dead friends in the little Anglican church above the sea.

Captain Martin Paulsen, fifty, First Mate Samuel Torkilson, twenty-four, and a Russian seaman named Gustav, of unknown age, were buried on October 11, 1896, in the cemetery behind the church. Wood from the wrecked ship was used to form an enclosure around the graves. In February 1897, when the body of a black cook and another unknown seaman were washed ashore, they too were buried within the enclosure. Bearing the captain's massive gold ring engraved with his wife's name, the two survivors left Neil's Harbour and returned to Norway, where they related a full account of the wreck and the kindness of the people at Neil's Harbour.

On the first anniversary of the wreck, J.E. Burchell, Vice-Consul of Sweden and Norway, presented a travelling communion set to Atkinson-Smith on behalf of the Norwegian king. The set is contained in a beautiful oak box and includes a paten, cruet and a gold enameled chalice set with rubies and pearls.

The chalice is engraved: "The Rev. Robert Atkinson-Smith, For Aedel Daad" (which means noble deed, the highest words of praise which any Norwegian monarch can bestow on a civilian).

Atkinson-Smith was later transferred to another parish, but upon his death, his widow presented the communion set to the bishop of the diocese who returned it to the parish of Neil's Harbour. It is still there today and is used by the incumbent to bring the sacrament of communion to anyone in his congregation unable to attend regular services.

The *Ariadne* was neither the first nor the last ship to founder near Neil's Harbour. The *Elizabeth*, a French topsail schooner manned by a Belgian crew, was wrecked in the same area in December 1918. The Belgians boarded at Neil's Harbour while they recovered from the mishap and during this time, it is said, saw their first snow.

The last shipwreck at Neil's Harbour occurred on July 29, 1921, when the *Volunda*, a 1,056-ton steel freighter under the command of Captain James Meskie, sailed into Neil's Harbour to get a better view of a house fire burning on the shore. The crew evidently paid more attention to events on land than to what was happening beneath their own ship. The vessel struck the rocks near the lighthouse and was wrecked.

Selected Shipwrecks from Cape North to Cape Smokey

Aranda: Built in 1924 by R. Duncan and Co. Ltd. in Glasgow, Scotland, *Aranda* had a gross tonnage of 1,547, dimensions of 253.8 by 39.2 by 17.4 feet, and wrecked south of Money Point in Aspy Bay on July 3, 1937.

Ariadne: A 782-ton Norwegian barque, she wrecked during a gale at MacKinnon's Point, near Green Cove, Ingonish, on October 7, 1896, while on a voyage from Grennock, Scotland, to Baie Verte, New Brunswick. Her port of registry was Oslo, Norway.

Aspy I: Ship Registration No. 122588. She was a 215-ton wooden passenger ferry built in 1909. The *Aspy I* wrecked in a

The *Carita* aground on Money Point, Cape Breton, in 1975.
(Photo: Shipsearch Marine)

storm on August 26, 1924, at Long Point, near Cape Egmont while on a voyage from White Point to Neil's Harbour. She was owned and operated by the North Shore Steamship Co.; her dimensions were 113 by 25 by 9 feet.

Auguste: A three-masted ship under the command of Captain Knowles, *Auguste* wrecked in a winter storm on November 15, 1761, while on a voyage to France. The *Auguste* was carrying many prominent and wealthy French passengers along with all their personal possessions from Quebec back to France.

Averill: The 1,690-ton British steamship *Averill* was wrecked on June 21, 1883, at Ingonish, Cape Breton, while on a voyage from Barrow, U.K., to Montreal with a cargo of steel rails. Built by W. Gray and Co. in 1878 and operated by the Christopher Furness Line, her dimensions were 260 by 34 by 23.1 feet and she was equipped with compound inverted engines.

Benona: The 1,357-ton British freighter *Benona* carrying coal from North Sydney to Montreal was wrecked on July 11, 1886, one mile south of the Cape North light. She was built in 1879 by the S.B. Whitehaven Co. and her dimensions were 240.2 by 33.2 by 17.3 feet.

Bessie Morris: The 1,729-ton British freighter *Bessie Morris* was wrecked in June, 1889, at White Point, Cape Breton, while on a voyage from Montreal to Sydney in ballast. She was built in

1880 by W. Hamilton and Co. and her dimensions were 280.2 by 34 by 21.9 feet.

Carita: Ship Registration No. 10730. Built as the *Ingrid Goriton,* the 4,053-ton Swedish freighter *Carita* was wrecked at Money Point on December 20, 1975. Her port of registry was Halsinborg, Sweden.

Fredrikka: The 448-ton wooden barque *Fredrikka* was on route from Le Havre, France, to Baie Verte, New Brunswick, when it wrecked during a storm in Aspy Bay on August 25, 1895.

Hungarian: The 1,612-ton iron schooner *Hungarian* wrecked at Cape North on July 2, 1897, due to a deviation with its compass. She was registered in Norway.

Kismet II: Built as the *Empire Lorenzo* in 1942 by W. Gray and Co. Ltd., West Hartlepool, U.K., she was renamed the *Baron Elcho* in 1946 and the *Kismet II* in 1955. On November 25, 1955, on a voyage from Philadelphia to Summerside, P.E.I., in ballast her steering gear became disabled and she went aground during a snowstorm at Cape North.

Lovland: The 2,389-ton Norwegian ship *Lovland,* sailing to Pugwash, Nova Scotia, went ashore on August 18, 1939, south of Money Point, Cape Breton, and became a total wreck. Built in 1907 by Short Brothers Ltd. in Sunderland, U.K., she was equipped with triple expansion engines and her dimensions were 295 by 45 by 19.6 feet.

Mercury: She wrecked near Black Brook, Ingonish, sometime in 1828 on a return voyage from Quebec with a cargo of wheat and oak timbers. The captain and crew walked to Aspy Bay, where they were rescued by William Daisley and taken to Sydney (except for one of their number who died and was buried at South Harbour beach). Daisley had a large fishing boat in which he engaged in the coastal trade, and several times he carried shipwrecked passengers to North Sydney.

Mary Bradford Pierce: She was a four-masted schooner of 1,133 gross tons built in 1919 at Boothbay, Maine, by the Atlantic Coast Co. On July 6, 1931, she went aground in thick fog at Cape Smokey Rocks. The vessel was underway in ballast from Eastport, Maine, for Campbellton, New Brunswick, to load a cargo of wood laths for New York City. The crew reached shore safely but

The *Mary Bradford Pierce* ashore on Cape Smokey Rocks.
(Photo: Shipsearch Marine)

the schooner was a total wreck. She was owned by Crowell and Thurlow; her dimensions were 198.3 by 39.2 by 18.8 feet, and her captain was J.D. Pierce.

Rouille: Ship Registration No. 156648. A tug boat that foundered off Cape Smokey on December 12, 1954, she was built at Collingwood, Ontario, and her port of registry was Toronto. Her dimensions were 100 feet long by 25 feet wide and she was 214 tons.

Sovereign: The English immigrant ship grounded and wrecked at Middle Harbour sometime in 1834. There is also a record of an unidentified ship wrecked at Middle Harbour in 1806 as well.

Volunda: Ship Registration No. 138658. The 1,056-ton steel freighter under the command of Captain James Meskie wrecked at Neil's Harbour on July 29, 1921, while on a voyage from North Sydney to Montreal. She was built at Trenton, Nova Scotia, in 1920, owned by Wasis Steamship Co., and her dimensions were 270 by 38.2 by 17.9 feet.

3

St. Paul Island
The Graveyard of the Gulf

Visibility was about ten miles and as clear as it was I could not see anything but open ocean, yet my eyes continued to strain looking at the long-range radar aboard the *Meg and Kel*. The target on the radar had grown larger and finally, two hours into our journey, I could see a fog bank. An hour later, as we approached the fog bank, a mountainous island with granite cliffs that reached hundreds of feet into the sky appeared to take shape and gradually materialized right in front of me.

The coastline that stood before me was one that commanded respect. Everywhere there were jagged rocks sticking out of the water like spears and they were surrounded by high cliffs made of sheer rock. Add to this the currents and the tides from the Gulf of St. Lawrence and you have before you a most treacherous piece of real estate. To make the situation appear even more mysterious, the entire island was shrouded in fog.

It was an eerie yet fitting introduction to St. Paul Island, the Graveyard of the Gulf. My adventure had begun a few hours earlier in Dingwall, a small fishing community in northern Cape

An aerial view of St. Paul Island (Photo by Billy Budge)

Breton Island. Our expedition team had assembled at the wharf of Aspy Bay Fisheries. After some brief introductions we proceeded to off-load the five vehicles that made up our caravan.

We had arranged for two large Cape Island fishing boats – the *Misty Dawn*, owned by Kelly Fitzgerald of Aspy Bay Fisheries and operated by Johnny and Paul Fitzgerald, and the *Meg and Kel*, owned and operated by Scott and Kim Fitzgerald. It had only taken two hours to load thirty-five dive gear bags, a portable compressor, 220 scuba tanks, boxes and boxes of food, supplies and dry goods, two Zodiac inflatable boats, two Yamaha outboard engines, and what certainly seemed like a never ending amount of underwater photo and video equipment. The expedition left the wharf in Dingwall at twelve noon, heading out on the last leg of a journey that for some of the passengers had started in London, England, forty-eight hours ago. We were twenty-two miles from our final destination; the trip would take three hours.

It was August 1, 1996, and we were sixteen British Sub Aqua Club (BSAC) divers from the U.K., one American photo journalist – Dave Millhouser – and a three-person support crew (myself, my dad Tommy Dwyer, and Jim Johnson, a professional diver and underwater photographer from Guysborough County). It was the first ever international expedition to St. Paul Island and while it would only last for seven days, my love affair and fascination with the island will last forever.

St. Paul Island
(Photo by H.W. Jones,
from the collection of
Don Young)

St. Paul Island is located approximately fourteen miles northeast of the northern tip of Cape Breton Island, Nova Scotia, and forty miles southwest of Cape Ray, Newfoundland, on Canada's east coast. This island is commonly referred to as the Graveyard of the Gulf and lies at the entrance to the Gulf of St. Lawrence, the gateway to Upper Canada. St. Paul is known to be the second most dangerous island in northeast Canada, possibly in all of northeast North America. Its layout is the complete opposite of the shifting sandy dunes of the most dangerous island – Sable Island.

Instead, razor sharp, jagged rocks, concealed by mist and swell, guard every approach to St. Paul. The island is only three miles long and one mile wide. It is mountainous with high cliffs and there are only two areas where a safe landing can be negotiated. The frigid water surrounding the island deepens quite rapidly near shore. The variable tidal streams and currents add to the danger arising from the ever-present fog. St. Paul Island is also subject to very dramatic and unpredictable weather. There are sudden rain and snow squalls and the wind can change direction without any warning as often as five times in one day. On most days throughout the year the entire island is shrouded in a blanket of haunting fog and mist. In short, this rocky outcrop can be a mariner's worst nightmare.

Early records seem to indicate that St. Paul Island was named by John Cabot in 1497. It may even have derived its name partially from Saint Paul who, while on his way to Rome as a prisoner, was shipwrecked on the island of Malta at a place known today as St. Paul's Bay. For this reason he is considered to be the patron saint of shipwrecked sailors. To the Mi'kmaq the name was and still is *Giogtao Menigog* (Round Island) and on a map of 1539, the Indian name *Gtjmegeite* was applied to St. Paul Island.

In preparation for the expedition I had gathered a vast amount of research. I obtained a great deal of information from the Campbell Journals at the Nova Scotia Archives. These journals were donated in 1996 by a descendant of Governor John Campbell. There are fourteen volumes covering day to day life on St. Paul Island from 1843 to 1921. Three generations of Campbells were born, lived and worked on this remarkable island for seventy-eight years. The southwest light was officially lit sometime in 1838. The management of the island was formally handed over to the Nova Scotia government and John Campbell was formally appointed governor. For nineteen years he faithfully performed his duties. Another excellent source of information is the diary of Frank L. Huntley, who was the southwest lightkeeper from January 1, 1916, to June 30, 1920.

I interviewed several former lighthouse keepers, salvage divers, fishermen and former Coast Guard people. I had compiled a great deal of research material on the history of St. Paul Island, and it was still very fresh in my mind as we made our way up the coast on the south side of the island.

St. Paul Island has an ominous history that is filled with events of unimaginable terror and disaster. There are more than 350 recorded shipwrecks and well over one thousand people buried on the island in unmarked graves. During the various waves of immigration, many immigrant ships, or "coffin ships" as they were called, en route from Ireland and England wrecked on the island. On board these packed vessels were hundreds of families and all their personal possessions. For many of them the promise of a New World meant an early grave. In the last three hundred years of seafaring, no one knows for sure how many additional ships simply disappeared or were wrecked on St. Paul Island with no one nearby to offer assistance, or even to know they had wrecked there.

The land surrounding Atlantic Cove (or Governor's Cove as it is sometimes called) on St. Paul would be a huge cemetery if tombstones marked all the graves that are actually there. Unfortunately, there are no such markers, or even crosses, left to identify the thousands who are buried there. If you look closely, however, there are some signs that indicate the presence of graves. A short distance to the northeast of Money Rocks and on somewhat higher ground a cemetery can be located, marked by the ruins of an old fence. Buried in this plot lie the remains of 202 passengers and crew from the British transport ship *Sovereign,* wrecked on the south side of the island at a place that now bears her name, Sovereign Cove, just a little north of Atlantic Cove.

Built in 1803, the 373-ton *Sovereign* wrecked on October 18, 1814. Two days later Captain Kirby of the transport ship *Champion* observed smoke on the island, which induced him to approach. When he observed signal flags of distress he hove to and relieved the destitute survivors of the *Sovereign*. The survivors arrived in Quebec on November 3. At the inquiry they stated that the ship was reduced to matchwood and went to pieces in ten minutes. Her master was S. Audus; owned by Barrack and Co., the *Sovereign* was en route from England to Quebec. The inquiry revealed that the *Sovereign* had onboard a very large and very precious cargo of Mexican silver dollars, being shipped to Quebec to pay soldiers.

The Quebec *Mercury* newspaper of Tuesday, November 8, 1814, reported: "The *Sovereign* sailed from Portsmouth on the 1st of September last under convoy of HMS *Zealous*. She had onboard 9 officers and 186 soldiers of the 49th 58th and 81st Regiments, 2 sergeants, 21 women and children, in all including the Captain, Mate and 19 seamen formed a total of 239 persons. Only 37 people were saved."

A map of St. Paul Island showing various shipwrecks.
(Photo courtesy of Don Young)

If you look closely at a map of St. Paul Island, very near where the southwest light now stands, there is a place called Jessie Cove, so named after the three-masted barque *Jessie* out of Three Rivers (Georgetown), Prince Edward Island, which wrecked during a violent snowstorm on January 1, 1824. Miraculously, eleven out of twenty-six of the crew and passengers survived the shipwreck. They managed to climb the jagged ice-covered rocks in a blinding snowstorm in sub-zero conditions and make their way to land, clutching what scarce provisions they could salvage from the wreck. In an attempt to attract the attention of people living in Cape North, on Cape Breton Island, the survivors built

41

great fires made from driftwood and wreckage night after night. A few saw these signals of distress, but they were powerless as heavy pack ice blocked the Gulf of St. Lawrence a few days after the ship went ashore. Hence no friendly vessel passed near the island until death had claimed them all.

The ship's owner, Donald MacKay, was onboard when the *Jessie* wrecked. MacKay kept a journal in which he recorded the harsh sufferings and tragic demise of the crew. (Part of this journal may be viewed today in the Historical Museum of Boston, Massachusetts, although how it got there remains a mystery.) The last entry was made on March 17, 1824, two and a half months after the *Jessie* had wrecked. MacKay was the last person to die. In a cruel twist of fate, eleven men had been saved from an ice-cold and watery grave only to die a more horrifying and unspeakable death from starvation and exposure while they waited for help that never came. What a private and personal hell each man must have gone through.

How the saga of the *Jessie* became known is even more remarkable. Throughout the early 1800s, usually in April of each year, French fishermen from Cheticamp and the Magdalen Islands went over the ice seal hunting. They used to call upon St. Paul Island to specifically salvage shipwrecks that may have occurred over the winter. A vessel from Cheticamp visited St. Paul and found the dead bodies of the crew of the *Jessie.* MacKay was wrapped in a richly made cloak and this was taken off the body. In the fall of that year one of the fishermen visited Charlotte-town, wearing MacKay's cloak. MacKay's widow met him on the street, recognized her husband's coat, pulled it open and inside found her husband's initials sewn in by her very own hand. She at once alerted the authorities and the fisherman was immediately arrested.

On his person was found 108 guineas of MacKay's money. The fisherman was able to explain satisfactorily to the authorities how he came into possession of the cloak and the money; he gave up all he had and was released. The widow immediately dispatched the schooner *Feronia* to St. Paul Island to recover any bodies. The crew succeeded in locating eleven bodies. They searched in vain for the remaining fifteen, but there was no trace of them. The bodies of MacKay and a Mr. McAlpin were wrapped in tarred sheets, deposited in coffins and placed onboard the *Feronia* for transport to Charlottetown. The crew of the *Feronia* then proceeded to bury the last remaining nine on the island, covering them with earth and sod, which they procured with great difficulty at a considerable distance.

The *Feronia* then called in at Margaree, where more of Mac-Kay's property was found, including a writing desk and numerous personal letters and bills salvaged from the wreck by persons unknown. On the *Feronia's* return to harbour at Charlottetown, the local newspaper reported that "The air crackled with excitement and large crowds of people assembled on the shore as a high breeze and flood tide brought the vessel up the river, her colours half mast high. She anchored opposite the residence of Donald MacKay, Esq., a cousin to the deceased, and in the course of the evening brought the bodies ashore."

Public outcry and demands were made for lighthouses but nothing was done in spite of countless disasters, some of astonishing proportions, and monthly stories making headlines in newspapers around the world. Fourteen more years would come to pass after the wreck of the *Jessie* before the Imperial Government of Canada would finally erect two lighthouses on St. Paul Island. In 1832, the governments of Nova Scotia and New Brunswick set up the first two official humane establishments or lifesaving stations on the island, one on the north side at Trinity Cove and one on the south side at Atlantic Cove.

But still the Graveyard of the Gulf reached out for more ships. On December 2, 1832, the 800-ton ship *Great Britain* – one of the largest merchant vessels sailing the St. Lawrence – bound from Quebec to Hull, England, was wrecked on the northeast side of the island. Out of a crew of thirty men only four succeeded in getting ashore. Three perished before they could be saved by people from the rescue station and only one man lived to tell the tale.

About fifty yards down the hill from the large house is a fairly flat stretch of land that reaches to the beach at Money Rocks. In this field lie the remains of more than four hundred Irish immigrants from the *Sibylle*, bound from Cromarty, Ireland, to Quebec and wrecked on September 11, 1832. It was said that in order to bury the dead, long trenches were dug and a mass burial was carried out. There were so many bodies washed ashore from the *Sibylle,* extra men were brought in from the mainland to partake in the gruesome recovery work and burial.

Three years later in 1835, St. Paul's reputation for its ship-killing capacity grew even more infamous as a violent storm raged through the Gulf of St. Lawrence and caused four ships to be wrecked on the island. As a result, over two hundred people perished in a single night. Some time in 1836 Hubert Aucoin was captain of a fishing smack out of Cheticamp, which was destroyed by ice during a seal hunt near St. Paul. In an attempt to save his own life he leaped onto an ice floe and eventually reached the island. His skeleton was found a few years later beside this inscription on a rock: "Hubert Aucoin, son of Anselme Aucoin, died of hunger and thirst. If you find my body, bury it." Ironically, in April 1842 his son was drowned in a sealing accident. It was a sad fact of life that many local families lost relatives in such mishaps.

In 1838 two lighthouses were finally erected on the island, one at the northeast tip and one at the southwest end. The main rescue station, stocked with provisions for shipwreck victims, was built in Atlantic Cove near the middle of the island. Even with a lighthouse on each end of the island, ships still continued to wreck there with an average of four recorded shipwrecks a year throughout the mid 1850s.

On the night of May 30, 1856, the 316-ton barque *Pallas,* sailing in dense fog at a speed of four-and-a-half knots, struck rocks on the southern side of St. Paul. The *Pallas* had left Cork, Ireland, for Quebec on April 28, 1856, with 136 immigrants onboard. They were asleep below when the ship hit. They rushed up on deck in such a state of panic that the ship's officers found it impossible to control them. They overcrowded the few available lifeboats, refusing to leave them when ordered to do so. As a result the lifeboats buckled under the weight and most of those in them were drowned. The captain prevailed on the crew and the rest of the immigrants to remain on the ship till daybreak when the remaining survivors were taken off in safety by rescue boats

The lifeboat crew stationed on St. Paul Island in the early 1900s.
(Photo by H.W. Jones from the collection of Don Young)

stationed on the island. The loss of life amounted to eighty-two people, of which seventy-nine were passengers.

In 1863, the steamer *Norwegian* went ashore on the south side of the island at the place which still bears her name – Norwegian Head. The *Norwegian* was the largest ship operated by the Allan Line. At the time of the disaster, she was under sail and steam, travelling at a rate of thirteen knots. She ran some distance on the shelving rock and in the morning fell over on her starboard side. By exceptional seamanship, skill and hard work, the lifesaving crew stationed on the island was able to save all five hundred of the passengers and crew, including a three-week-old infant and an eighty-year-old-man. The sails from the *Norwegian* were salvaged and used to build a makeshift tent city to house the survivors in Atlantic Cove. Our 1996 British Sub Aqua Club expedition pitched our tents in that same field 133 years later.

On June 26, 1872, the *Adalia* of London under Captain Sanderson, bound to Quebec with general cargo and a hundred passengers, went ashore in the fog on the south side of St. Paul. The crew and passengers were safely landed. The steamship *Pictou* arrived at daylight on June 30 and its captain communicated immediately with Captain Sanderson. At 7 a.m. they commenced

Samuel Cunard Campbell
and the lifeboat crew in the
early 1900s.
(H.W. Jones photo from the
collection of Don Young)

embarking passengers and baggage, and finished at 12:30 p.m. *Pictou* then proceeded at once for Quebec.

The *Adalia* was lying on the rocks, with her stern about four-teen feet under water and her bow entirely out of the water. A good part of the cargo was saved and handed out of the forehold. The captain and crew remained on St. Paul Island to save all that was possible. A group of "wreckers" attempted to plunder the ship, but they were beaten off by the crew and passengers with firearms. The captain expected further trouble as he also noticed that several schooners were hovering about near the island. While the lighthouses on the island were immune to disasters, the ships that supplied them were not.

In 1874 the Canadian government lighthouse supply schoo-ner *La Canadienne* was wrecked near Trinity Cove on the north-west side of St. Paul Island. *La Canadienne*, built in Quebec in 1855, was 101 tons and measured ninety-two feet in length.

With the first recorded shipwreck on Cape Breton Island occurring in 1597 and the first rescue station ever built on St. Paul Island in 1832, there remains 235 years of shipping and shipwrecks to account for. How many people are actually buried

Atlantic Cove in the 1920s
showing buildings which housed the lifeboat crews and their families.
(H.W. Jones photo from the collection of Don Young)

on the island in unmarked graves will remain a mystery. From information and research currently available we do in fact know that well over 1,000 people are buried there. Most were immigrants trying to start a new life with their families. Some were soldiers on their way to war; some were on their way home from war. Some were passengers on a voyage of discovery to a new land, and some were captains and crew who ultimately and unwillingly gave their lives working their chosen trade. From what I have read conducting research on St. Paul Island, I cannot adequately put into words the sheer amount of terror, suffering, misery and hardships these people must have experienced.

In 1914 a large house was built in Atlantic Cove to accommodate the lifesaving crew and their families. In 1924, three more buildings were erected to house radio equipment, a power plant and an Officer in Charge of the station. In December of 1925 the lifesaving station was officially closed and abandoned. It was considered that with modern lighthouses and now a wireless station, any further wrecks of note were highly improbable. In 1962 the original wooden lighthouse on the northeast side of the island was replaced with a white concrete tower that still stands today. In 1991 St. Paul Island had the dubious honour of being the last lighthouse in eastern Canada to be automated.

The loud roar of our diesel engine dropped to a quiet roar, and I was suddenly snapped back to reality. We had arrived at Atlantic Cove. We anchored in the centre of the cove and began to shuttle our supplies and passengers ashore in Zodiacs. Once ashore in true expedition style, we had to scale a thirty-foot cliff, cross through three hundred feet of grassy field then climb another hundred-foot steep hill. Our base camp was set up near the site of the old lifesaving station. The former Royal Canadian Air Force residence building is still standing overlooking pictur-esque Atlantic Cove. The island is covered with a very dense jun-gle-like growth of short trees and has two freshwater lakes and a pond. However, the water is not drinkable and has been stagnant for quite some time.

Our first dive was at Five Sided Cove on the north side of the island where we explored the remains of the *Victoria*, a French fishing trawler that wrecked in the late 1950s and was the last official shipwreck to occur on St. Paul. This wreck starts in thirty feet of crystal clear water and stops at ninety feet. It is spread out over a very large area and there is still a lot of the ship to see. Her engine is still remarkably intact, complete with a gauge panel and manufacturer's plate. A huge anchor and miles of chain make for some interesting video. There are winches, bollards, deck plates, pieces of the hull and a massive debris field that would easily occupy four dives at the very least just to see it all.

The wreck is teeming with marine life. Visibility then was between forty and sixty feet in the shallow section, while the deeper parts of the wreck offered over a hundred feet of visibility in all directions. Water temperature was an inviting 60° Fahren-heit on the surface, followed by a distinct thermocline at twenty-five feet and ending up at 30° Fahrenheit at eighty feet. Water temperature changes with depth, generally getting colder as you descend. While descending, you may encounter an abrupt tran-sition to distinctly cold water. This is called a thermocline. The temperature difference may be as great as 15 to 20° Fahrenheit. Sometimes you can even see visual distortion at the thermocline that looks like the shimmering you see rising from a hot asphalt road. This effect is caused by the mixing of two temperature layers.

Our team logged several dives on this site, and then we went looking for the *Chelston*, which we had on good advice was wrecked nearby. We started our dive in ninety feet of water, swimming along a ledge. From this vantage point we could see down into huge crevices and canyons. With more than a hundred feet of visibility we were able to cover a large area, finding lots of wreckage and evidence of many wrecks. We located the remains of the *Chelston* a few days later.

We spent the next few days diving on the southeast side of the island. At a place on the chart called Aurora Rocks, named after the *Aurora* wrecked in the early 1800s, we found several wrecks. On our first dive we found a debris field full of wreckage: boilers, large pieces of steel plates, anchors and chain, propellers and all kinds of structure. Underwater visibility was averaging seventy-five feet in all directions. While I was filming the wreckage a school of herring surrounded the divers and the wreck, swirling around us for most of the dive. The marine life on St. Paul Island is as impressive as it is vibrant. There are cunners, perch, flounder, wolf fish, large crabs, lobster, and the occasional resident lump fish. In total we dived three different wrecks at the entrance to Atlantic Cove. Preliminary research indicated that there are twenty-eight different ships wrecked in this cove alone.

The 1996 British Sub Aqua Club expedition spent six days diving and only explored eight different shipwrecks, a very small sampling of what St. Paul has to offer. During the week we hiked old trails and paths and we visited a forgotten grave site, the final resting place of five-and-a-half-month-old twins. Eric George Laing and Violet May Laing were born February 20, 1938. The headstone reads: "Eric George & Violet May, twin babies of Geo. & Mary Laing, Died August 1938." The cause of death was dysentery caused by unsanitary conditions – the previous occupants of the house emptied their bedpans into the coal bin during the winter, instead of the approved disposal site. The children's parents did not discover the source of the bacteria until it was too late. Over the years former lightkeepers and visiting Boy Scouts from Truro, Nova Scotia, have kept up the grave site, and even today it looks remarkably peaceful and well-kept as it overlooks Hay Cove on the south side of the island.

Make no mistake, diving on St. Paul Island is physically demanding, strenuous and at times psychologically challenging. The water surrounding the island is ice-cold; currents are strong and ever present. Diving here is very much a team effort and it requires discipline, experience, skill and commitment. You are totally dependent on the team and on a chase boat (Zodiac) to pick you up after a dive. There is no shore diving from the island, only boat diving and this type of diving is not for everyone. Then there are the logistics of actually getting to and from the island. Because of the island's location in the Gulf of St. Lawrence, it can only be reached and dived safely during the months of July, August and September. A journey to St. Paul Island will take six hours by highway (Halifax to Dingwall), then a further three hours by boat (one way) out to the island.

Once, on a return trip to the mainland, the weather turned bad and it took us five hours to make port. During another expedition, a sudden and violent rainstorm engulfed our dive boat, the *Meg and Kel,* and during the night the wind changed direction five times. Our three huge anchors dragged and in a matter of minutes we were almost on the rocks. In the dead of a pitch black night, with the sea raging all around us, we had to cut our lines with a fire axe, abandon our anchorage and make a run for the north side of the island. Minutes passed like hours as the *Meg and Kel* battled mountainous waves, high winds and heavy rain for the two hours that it took to find shelter there.

The next morning the people in our base camp awoke to find us gone and with no way to contact us by radio as the radio signal was blocked by the mountains. They had no idea what happened to us so they were very happy to see us steaming back into Atlantic Cove later that morning.

That night served as a harsh reality check and a constant reminder to stay alert. Suffice to say, I remember feeling very religious when I went ashore the next morning.

Be advised that St. Paul Island is not an island to be taken lightly. If the unpredictable weather turns on you, it can be a hellish place. The locals in Dingwall have an expression they use to describe St. Paul Island: "It can be heaven or it can be hell." The logistical requirements are formidable and planning for an expedition of any size or magnitude takes months.

Today, if you examine a map of St. Paul Island, you will find that nearly every place on the map is named after a shipwreck. Norwegian Head, Viceroy Cove, Jessie Cove, Sovereign Cove, Isabella Cove, Glencoe Cove, Brunett Cove, Moon Point, Barbara Rocks, Aurora Rocks, and Money Rocks (where the bodies from many wrecks washed in) are all so named after the shipwrecks that have occurred there.

For intrepid explorers, wreck divers and underwater photographers, the prize for challenging the elements and braving the logistics is underwater visibility that often exceeds a hundred feet in all directions and an enormous untapped potential for the discovery and exploration of virgin shipwrecks. Divers visiting St. Paul will experience the unprecedented opportunity to view first-hand a seabed littered with the broken bones and remains of hundreds of forgotten shipwrecks. On subsequent dives we have found huge pieces of steel ships in the form of boilers, engines, steel plates, anchors, propellers, etc. We also discovered cannons, cannon balls, bronze spikes, deadeyes (round wooden blocks with grooved circumferences used to fasten the sails of a ship), and other pieces of old wooden wrecks from the 1700s. There is no shortage of things to do and see on St. Paul; you need only walk the trails or explore the coastline to see some spectacular sites. The island is, without question, quite beautiful and very picturesque.

In August 2000, I was leading a team of visiting divers from the Newbury Sub Aqua Club in the U.K. We were exploring the north side of St. Paul Island when Mick Cullen and I made an incredible discovery. In forty-five feet of water we found bronze spikes and large bronze pins. A second team started exploring deeper and at ninety feet they found large and small deadeyes. At 110 feet diver Robin Adams sighted a large bronze ship's bell dated 1861, which bore the name *Clymene*.

One year later I was part of a week-long underwater archae-ological survey that was being carried out complete with a site map, still photographs and underwater video by yet another group of visiting U.K. divers. Our preliminary research indicated that the *Clymene* was built in 1851 by Messrs. Peile, Scott and Co., in Workington, England. Her registration number was 10562 and she was an East Indiaman, clipper-built flush ship, which meant that the cabin and forecastle accommodations were all between decks.

The *Clymene* had two decks and three masts. Rigged with a standing bowsprit, she was square-sterned, caravel built, and had a woman figurehead gracing her bow. She registered 826 tons, was 157 feet long, had a breadth of thirty-one feet and a depth of hold of twenty-two feet. She was coppered and copper-fastened. She spent the first twenty-three years of her life sailing from her home port of Liverpool, England, to Calcutta, India, and various other parts of the Indian Ocean.

Further research eventually produced the names of the crew members, various owners and captains right up until July 1874, when *Clymene* was listed on the Lloyds of London Shipping Register as being "Sold Foreign." We were at a complete loss so we started to research St. Paul Island. Of the more than 350 ship-wrecks that are known to be on the island, we were astounded to find there was no evidence or research indicating a shipwreck named *Clymene.*

There was, however, a ship named the *Anna* that matched the same description and was wrecked in the same area as the *Clymene* in 1874. Subsequent research indicated that the *Clymene* was sold to J.J. Ekman in Gothenburg, Sweden, and was renamed the *Anna* in July 1874. Later in September of 1874 the *Anna* wrecked on Goat Rock on the north side of St. Paul Island. The *Anna* was in ballast en route to New York at the time. This was recently confirmed by the curator of the National Museum in Sweden.

The mystery of the date on the bell has led researchers to believe at some point around 1861 the original bell, which would have been dated 1851, was lost or damaged beyond repair and a new bell was commissioned in 1861. When the *Clymene* was "sold foreign" in 1874, the ship's name was changed to *Anna*, but the original ship's bell with the original name was kept as is, as was a common practice in those days. In 2002 the bell was recovered by parties unknown. Fortunately, it was eventually donated to our museum in Dingwall, and we in turn loaned it to the Nova Scotia Museum of Natural History in Halifax.

It's hard to imagine what future expeditions are going to discover. The ice-cold water's preservative qualities make St. Paul Island a virtual time capsule of marine technology. It is a place where nature has remained undefeated. The contrasts are stark, the beauty is unsurpassed and it appears today almost exactly as it must have appeared three hundred years ago.

The underwater and surface photo/video opportunities are extraordinary. A one-week expedition to St. Paul Island will allow the participant between eighteen and twenty-one spectacular dives. We saw eagles, porpoises and whales every day we were there. For those of you who are up for a great adventure and a chance to dive into history, you will not be disappointed. Over the last eight years I have logged over one hundred dives on St. Paul Island and I have only explored 25 percent of the island's coast.

For sheer adventure and excitement I highly recommend a visit to St. Paul Island and if you are up for it, an "expedition." To me, some of the greatest personal rewards an expedition experience can offer a person are adventure and camaraderie. For me and my companions lifelong memories and friendships were forged by overcoming obstacles as a team. As a member of an expedition team each of us faced challenging situations with new friends, we shared the risks and sometimes we braved the dangers together. It was all part of the expedition experience.

These days very few people ever get the opportunity to visit St. Paul Island. However, if you like shipwreck diving where the water is cold but crystal clear, then a day trip, a weekend or maybe even a one-week expedition to St. Paul Island is for you. Make no mistake, the diving is spectacular, but it is a privilege that must be earned. If you want to experience your own personal adventure in real time, then take an unforgettable journey to St. Paul Island. I guarantee you, it will be a once in a lifetime experience that you will never forget.

Today St. Paul Island is in a state of decline. The island once boasted magnificent turn-of-the-century houses, a post office and even a lobster factory. Only a handful of these houses and buildings are still standing today. Nonetheless, rich in history, folklore and mystery, St. Paul Island still beckons divers to its coastline. Some say it still holds the key to much unfound treasure and yet-to-be-discovered history.

Selected Shipwrecks on St. Paul Island

Adalia: A steamship of 1,270-tons, Adalia had a length of 232 feet and a beam of 32 feet, iron construction and a speed of nine knots. Built by William Doxford of Sunderland, U.K., in 1864, *Adalia* was owned by the London and Charleston Steamship Co. The London Line ran between London, Plymouth and Quebec. The structure was complex; British Colonial SS Co., Temperley Line, and London Line were names used at different times while many passenger manifests in the National Archives of Canada are coded WW, apparently from Wilcocks and Weekes, the Plymouth agents. The *Adalia* was under Captain Sanderson bound to Quebec from Liverpool, U.K., with general cargo and a hundred passengers when she went ashore in the fog on June 26, 1872, on the south side of St. Paul Island.

Alfred Taylor: This twenty-ton ship wrecked sometime in 1904.

Anna: Originally the *Clymene,* this 3-masted 746-ton ship sailed from Sweden and wrecked on September 8, 1874, off Goat Rock on the north side of the island.

Anna B: This sixteen-ton schooner collided with another ship and wrecked March 5, 1889.

Annie F. Hartigan: Ship Registration No. 142970. Formerly the 38-ton schooner *Victoria Kendall,* she was built in Morrisville, Newfoundland, in 1920. In November 1933 the damaged fishing schooner limped into Atlantic Cove and sank four hours later.

Arcola: Ship Registration No. 108250. Built by William Thomson and Co. in 1897, she was owned and operated by W. Gray and Co. She was 2,599 tons, 314 by 44.1 by 20.7 feet and equipped with triple expansion engines. This British steamship was wrecked on July 9, 1908, in Hay Cove while sailing in ballast to Chatham, New Brunswick.

Aurora: Very little is known about the SS *Aurora*, but it is believed to have been wrecked some time in 1903 near the entrance to Atlantic Cove. It was carrying a cargo of steel rails and it was discovered by Ed Barrington of Offshore Diving and Salvage in 1972.

Barbara: This 229-ton brig from the U.K. wrecked on April 5, 1878, near the Southwest light.

Briton Elliot: This vessel wrecked near the Aurora Rocks.

Briton: A wooden ship under the command of a Captain Dixon, the *Briton* wrecked on the northeast side of the island on January 2, 1831, while on a voyage from Miramichi, New Brunswick, to London, England, with a cargo of lumber. Only one survived from a crew of eighteen people. Her port of registry was Whitby, U.K.

Brodrene: This 464-ton Norwegian barque struck Anchor Rock on May 26, 1896, and sank almost immediately, but not before the entire crew was saved and put ashore at Atlantic Cove.

Brunette: This barque wrecked sometime in July of 1844 at Brunette Cove.

Canada: This brig under the command of Captain Parks wrecked on May 8, 1826, on the northeast side of the island while on a voyage from Belfast, Ireland, to Quebec. Her Port of Registry was Aberdeen, Scotland.

Canadienne: Ship Registration No. 073495. A 51-ton, two-masted wooden schooner built at House Harbour, Quebec, in 1883, the *Canadienne* wrecked on the northeast end of the island on October 26, 1908. She was owned by Cyriac, Simeon and Norbert La France and her dimensions were 62.5 by 20.2 by 8 feet.

Chelston: Ship Registration No. 119444. The British cargo ship *Chelston* was wrecked on St. Paul Island on September 12, 1919, on a voyage from Chatham, New Brunswick, to Glasgow, Scotland, with a cargo of lumber. Built by the Waverley Shipping Co. in 1904, she weighed 3,687-tons, was 347.4 by 51 by 24.2 feet and equipped with triple expansion steam engines.

Cornelia: This barque wrecked May 15, 1872.

Deodata: This vessel wrecked at Trinity Cove.

Devonshire: An 858-ton sailing ship from the U.K. under the command of Captain Henry Dinning, *Devonshire* wrecked on June 5, 1870, while on a voyage from Liverpool, U.K., to Quebec. She was built in 1860 in Quebec and her dimensions were 162 by 35 by 21feet.

Doris V. Douglas: This vessel wrecked October 27, 1954.

Duncan: This wooden vessel registered in Hull, U.K., wrecked at Hay Cove, just a little north of Atlantic Cove sometime in 1827.

Elliott: Ship Registration No. 97076. Built in 1903, the *Elliott* was out of Channel, Newfoundland, and had 115 men onboard. On March 17, 1904, the steamer was jammed in ice and sank in Atlantic Cove. Every man was taken safely ashore by the island's alert lifesaving boat crew.

Elliott Heste: This 227-ton schooner wrecked in Atlantic Cove March 26, 1903.

Emperor: A 625-ton barque wrecked in a snow storm at Goat Cove on November 27, 1871, the *Emperor* was on a voyage from Quebec to Bristol, U.K. Sixteen people were lost.

Enchantress: This ship sailed from Bristol, U.K. under the command of Captain Findlater and wrecked at Trinity Cove on September 23, 1848.

England's Queen: This ship wrecked May 11, 1847.

Eudora: Ship Registration No. 038227. This 708-ton barque was built in Meteghan, Nova Scotia, in 1862. The *Eudora* was under the command of Captain Wentworth Killam when she wrecked on September 21, 1866, while on a voyage from Ardossan, Scotland, to Quebec. Her dimensions were 146.5 by 33.9 by 19 feet.

Freeman: This ship wrecked sometime in May 1820, en route from Greenock, U.K., to Pictou, Nova Scotia.

George Barclay: This brig wrecked on January 1, 1838.

Glenroe: Ship Registration No. 69436. This 569-ton barque was built at Port Phillip, Nova Scotia, in 1875; it wrecked on June 5, 1876.

Great Britain: While on a voyage from Quebec to Hull, U.K., the *Great Britain* (at the time one of the largest sailing ships in the world) wrecked on December 2, 1833, near Trinity Cove on the northwest side of the island. She had a crew of twenty-nine people, of which four made it ashore. Three later died on the island and only one person survived.

Harlaw: Ship Registration No. 084354. The *Harlaw* was built in 1881 at Glasgow, Scotland. She was 267 registered tons and measured 165 by 24.5 by 11.8 feet. A government report from the Department of Marine and Fisheries dated April 8, 1911, stated the *Harlaw* was first seen on the afternoon of April 4 approaching St. Paul Island. On the morning of April 7, the keeper at the Northeast Light reported the *Harlaw* was steering in to the shore ice on the north side of the island. The ship was at the edge of the shore ice and the crew was getting their provisions ashore. The captain reported that the ship first sustained damage from floating ice on March 25 and again on the 27th. Five hours after the crew left the ship on April 7 she sank at a location one mile north of the island. The *Harlaw*, a sealing vessel at the time, was owned and operated by Pickford & Black Steamship Co.

Heron: This 283-ton barque wrecked on the island on May 26, 1872, while on a voyage from Bordeaux, France, to Quebec.

Horatio: This wooden vessel from the U.K. under the command of a Captain Peart wrecked on the island on May 23, 1826.

Hunter: This ship wrecked some time in 1835.

Irishman: This immigrant ship on a voyage to Quebec from Ireland, wrecked on the island sometime in early 1834.

Isabella: Wrecked on St. Paul Island in the early spring of 1834, the *Isabella* was bound for Montreal from Workington, U.K., with 130 immigrants. Seven drowned and the remainder suffered great distress.

James: Also wrecked on St. Paul Island in the early spring of 1834, the *James* was under the command of Captain Crooks and bound for Montreal from Workington, U.K., with immigrants.

James A. McKean: This schooner wrecked on October 30, 1878.

Jane: This brig wrecked at Anchor Rocks on May 7, 1834, while on a voyage from the U.K. to Quebec. The survivors were picked up by a passing vessel and taken to Quebec.

Jessie: The three-masted barque *Jessie* out of Prince Edward Island wrecked on St. Paul Island during a violent snowstorm on January 1, 1823.

John and Charlotte: This vessel wrecked sometime in 1822.

Judique: Ship Registration No. 9016282. This 22-ton schooner was built in Arichat, Cape Breton, in 1829 and wrecked in 1841.

Jupiter: This wooden sailing vessel wrecked at Jupiter Cove sometime in May 1767.

La Canadiane: In 1874 the Canadian government lighthouse supply schooner was wrecked near Trinity Cove on the northwest side of St. Paul Island. Built in Quebec in 1855, the schooner was 101 tons and measured 92 feet in length.

Margret: This Irish immigrant ship wrecked sometime in 1834 on the south side of the island.

Maria Casapona: A 624-ton barque out of Italy wrecked in dense fog near the southwest light on October 13, 1897, while on a voyage from Miramichi, New Brunswick, to Spain.

Mary: This brig under the command of Captain Harrison from the U.K. on a voyage to Miramichi, New Brunswick, wrecked in dense fog on July 20, 1834.

Mary Patricia: Ship Registration No. 150246. This 52-ton steamer, formerly a World War I minesweeper out of Halifax, wrecked on September 7, 1930. She was built in Montreal in 1917 and her dimensions were 84 feet long and 19 feet wide.

Mette Margrethe: This 429-ton barque was on a voyage in ballast from Sauwig, Norway, to Miramichi, New Brunswick, when it wrecked at Little Harbour near the southwest light in dense fog on July 5, 1881. She was built in 1813 and five people were lost when she wrecked.

Miner: Ship Registration No. 038232. The 650-ton Yarmouth ship *Miner*, went aground in Glencoe Cove on August 24, 1863. The daring members of the lifesaving station brought all the passengers and crew safely ashore. She was owned by Thomas Killam, at the time a member of the House of Commons representing Yarmouth County, and her dimensions were 147 by 30 by 19 feet.

Minerva: This 1,364-ton ship was on a voyage from Liverpool, U.K., to Quebec when it became stranded in thick fog and wrecked at Whistle Point on September 15, 1871.

Mitchell: A wooden schooner, the *Mitchell* wrecked at West Point on St. Paul Island sometime in the 1800s.

Moon: This barque from the U.K. wrecked on May 8, 1834, at Moon Point. The survivors were eventually rescued by a passing vessel bound for Quebec.

Noon: An immigrant ship out of Sunderland, U.K., commanded by Captain Phillips, the *Noon* wrecked on St. Paul Island in the early spring of 1834.

Norwegian: Ship Registration No. 33537. This four-decked iron barque was built in Dumbarton, Scotland, in 1861. She was 2,450 gross tons and measured 301 feet in length by 17 feet wide. On June 14, 1863, the Allan steamer *Norwegian* went ashore on the south side of the island which still bears her name

Ocean Belle: Ship Registration No. 41662. This 49-ton wooden schooner, built in Antigonish, N.S., in 1859, was wrecked while salvaging the wreck of the *Minerva* sometime in July 1873.

Olivette: Ship Registration No. 83230. A 268-ton brigantine built in Bideford, Prince Edward Island, in 1881, the *Olivette* was en route to England when it wrecked on May 25, 1886.

Pallas: This 316-ton barque was built in 1826 by Clifton and Co. of New Brunswick, the *Pallas* with 136 immigrants plus crew left Cork, Ireland, for Quebec on April 28, 1856. She struck on the rocks on the southern side of St. Paul Island.

Rajahgopaul: This sailing ship from the U.K. wrecked September 4, 1870.

Ratchel: This ship was wrecked on April 17, 1847, on the south side of the island.

Rippler: This 600-ton barque was wrecked on November 27, 1871, while on a voyage from Montreal, Quebec, to Cork, Ireland.

Seaflower: Ship Registration No. 9027925. The 48-ton wooden schooner/supply vessel, under the command of Captain Florian, wrecked at Trinity Cove, near West Point on St. Paul Island in May 24, 1844. She was built in Shippagan, New Brunswick, in 1839 and her dimensions were 52 by 15 by 8 feet.

Sebastopol: This barque from the U.K. was wrecked on May 17, 1880.

Scandanavia: This Norwegian sailing ship was wrecked June 5, 1870.

Shark: This brig wrecked sometime in 1820.

Sibylle: Bound from Cromarty, Ireland, to Quebec, the *Sibylle* wrecked on St. Paul Island on September 11, 1832. More than 400 Irish immigrants died and were buried in mass graves near Atlantic Cove.

Sovereign: Built in 1803, the 373-ton British transport ship *Sovereign* was carrying a large consignment of Spanish American silver coins from England bound for Quebec when it wrecked on October 18, 1814. Her master was S. Audus and she was owned by the Barrick Company. On board were nine officers, and 186 solders of the 49th, 58th and the 81st Regiments, two servants and twenty-one women and including her crew 239 persons in all. Only thirty-seven people survived.

St. Petersburg: This vessel wrecked at Brunette Cove on the south side of the island.

Teazer: The 82-ton American steamer *Teazer* was built in 1905 and was crushed in the ice and wrecked near the island on March 26, 1948.

Thistle: Ship Registration No. 092346. This 114-ton schooner wrecked in fog near Atlantic Cove on May 28, 1902, while on a voyage from North Sydney to Quebec.

Trinity C: This vessel was wrecked at Trinity Cove on the northwest side of the island.

Turret Bay: Ship Registration No. 104245. This British steamship was built by the Canadian Ocean and Inland Navigation Co. in 1894. She was owned and operated by W. Doxford and Sons. At 2,211 tons, 297 by 40 by 21.7 feet, and equipped with triple expansion engines the *Turret Bay* ran onto a submerged rock off St. Paul Island, backed off and sank in deep water on May 21, 1904. She was on a voyage to Montreal with a cargo of coal. The captain and eleven others were drowned.

Tuscarora: Ship Registration No. 145543. A Great Lakes steel package freighter owned and operated by the Lehigh Transportation Co., the 2,386-ton steamship was built by Globe Iron Works in Cleveland, Ohio, in 1890. Her dimensions were 306.8 by 40 by 25.6 feet; her hull number was 32. In 1917 the *Tuscarora* was cut in two at Buffalo Dry Dock Co., Buffalo, New York, and reassembled afloat at Montreal, Quebec. The *Tuscarora* was requisitioned by the United States Shipping Board for World War I off-lakes use. It left Montreal December 6, 1917, with a crew of thirty and on December 9 went aground on the southwest side of St. Paul Island with all hands lost. Eleven days later on December 20, 1917, Frank H. Huntley, the southwest light keeper on St. Paul Island, recovered a waterlogged lifeboat and also observed lots of wreckage.

Vanguard: This barque, under the command of Captain Thomas B. Rose, wrecked on Aurora Rocks on May 24, 1845, while on a voyage from Whitby, U.K., to Miramichi, New Brunswick.

Viceroy: This vessel wrecked sometime in September 1885 at Viceroy Cove, en route to Liverpool with a cargo of lumber.

Victoria: A French diesel fishing trawler launched January 15, 1928, by Burmeister and Wain Ltd., Copenhagen, for Société Nouvelle des Pecheries a Vapeur of Arcachon, France, she was the fastest and biggest diesel trawler afloat. Her dimensions were 208.8 by 32.9 by 18.7 feet. The *Victoria* wrecked on St. Paul Island on April 28, 1953, and at the time of her sinking she was owned by M.A. Glatre of France. The *Victoria* had the dubious honour of being the last official shipwreck to occur on St. Paul Island.

Warwick: This vessel wrecked between Jupiter Cove and MacDougall Cove on the north side of the island.

Wild Wave: Ship Registration No. 36824. This 453-ton wooden barque was built in Cascumpec, P.E.I., in 1860. The *Wild Wave* was wrecked at West Point on the north side of St. Paul Island on September 7, 1870, while on a voyage from Quebec to Swansea, Wales.

There are more than 350 known shipwrecks on St. Paul Island and it simply is not possible to list them all. There is also so much research information on St. Paul Island available that several books could be written on the subject.

4

Scatarie Island

A mile off the coast of picturesque Main-A-Dieu Harbour just a little north of Louisbourg in eastern Cape Breton, Nova Scotia, lies an island with a remarkable history. The island is seven miles long and three miles across at its widest point. The name appears as Scatori on a map from 1656. Many historians speculate that it is of Portuguese origin, perhaps a transformation of the name St. Catherine. Scatarie was also called Whale Island and Wolf Island during the late 1600s and early 1700s.

The waters surrounding Scatarie are considered to be as dangerous a threat to mariners as St. Paul Island, Seal Island (in the Bay of Fundy near Clark's Harbour in southwest Nova Scotia) and Sable Island. Its reefs and massive shoals extend out as far as one mile in some places, and much of the time the island is whipped by rough seas and high winds or shrouded in a dense fog. In July 1798, H.M. Sloop of War *Rover*, fourteen guns, sailed from Halifax for Sydney with Lieutenant General Ogilvie and his staff. On the evening of the third day, while sailing before a nine knot breeze, she struck an outside reef off Scatarie. Owing to the thorough discipline maintained in the emergency, all hands with the exception of one man were landed safely on the island. A short time after the ship went to pieces.

Names like Hatchet Rock Cove, Ragged Rock Cove and Savage Cove do, in fact, accurately describe the island's infamous and lethal coastline. Other parts of the island are named after shipwrecks that have occurred there over the past three hundred years: places like Secret Cove, named after the brig *Secret*, wrecked there in 1841, and the Columbo Breakers, named after the British cargo ship *Columbo*, wrecked there on July 9, 1885. The *Columbo* was on a voyage from Bull River, South Carolina, to Dublin with a cargo of phosphate rock when she wrecked on the northeast side of Scatarie Island.

The island was first settled in 1713 and by 1752 it was home to 106 people. The first lighthouse was erected in 1839 at the northeastern tip of the island. Most of the wood used to build the lighthouse was brought in by sailing vessel, but the spars of many wrecked ships were used as structural members. The lighthouse was equipped with a foghorn and was used as a rescue station until the 1920s. In 1942 twelve families were living on the island. They had their own church and school, and had formed a cooperative society with fishing as their main industry. The original lighthouse tower was eventually replaced with a steel skeleton tower with an enclosed stairwell. Located seventy-four feet above sea level, the lantern in the new tower is visible for up to fourteen miles.

Of particular interest to divers, Scatarie Island has intrigued us with its countless shipwrecks. History records Scatarie playing small, but sometimes crucial, roles in five wars that spanned three hundred years. She has claimed ships and men from all nations. Divers have been visiting the wrecks off Scatarie since the late 1800s. Over the years the list of divers and diving expeditions grew. While some were successful, most were not. Towards the mid 1960s, diving activity increased and in the early 1970s the Cape Breton Development Corporation (DEVCO) sponsored a project to research the shipwrecks and history of Scatarie Island in preparation for a "Scuba Tourism" development project.

The original 1974 report compiled by the DEVCO expedition entitled "The Dive Scatarie Project" was never released to the public, and even today, it remains elusive and surrounded by controversy. Many years ago I acquired a copy of this secret report. It tells an incredible and fascinating story of the project. The report is more than fifty pages long and is broken up into two parts with twenty-seven sections. The following is a brief review of various sections in the report, including quotations taken directly from the report.

Objectives of the Report: "The objectives laid down for the project, which became known as Dive Scatarie, were to search as much as possible of the inshore waters of Scatarie Island, to accurately plot and record what was visible in the way of wrecks, marine life or other things of interest to divers."

Points of Interest: "It was searching for land evidence that helped us piece together the stories of three different shipwrecks, . . . believe[d] to be a very important part of our early Canadian history. As a result of these three shipwrecks almost 1,000 people perished."

Tourist Development: "Tourism potential resulting from the Dive Scatarie Project is nothing short of tremendous. This year saw more diving parties visit Scatarie Island than any other part of Cape Breton including Louisbourg."

Material Found (not on a wreck site): "Another area revealed clay pipes which were traced back to the Dutch occupation of Cape Breton. Some were brought back to the surface for further study. According to the experts from Louisbourg, the only other specimens of clay pipes such as those found at Scatarie were discovered when the National Geographic Diving Team explored the ruins of Port Royal in the Caribbean."

Condition of Material Found: "Finding such perfect specimens as the clay pipes and lead shot tells us that it may be possible to find other artifacts in near original state. It should also be noted that the experts on ancient wreckage from Louisbourg were surprised to see these items so well preserved."

Map of Wreck Sites: "It should be noted that an accurate chart must be produced if it is to benefit future plans for diving at Scatarie and surrounding areas."

Catalogue of Findings: "The divers have located the remains of fifty ships at least, but the remains are so broken up and mixed that identification is unlikely. At least 100 cannons and a complete arsenal of projectiles are available apart from other interesting items. There is enough iron, lead, copper and bronze for a major salvage operation.

"The island is the meeting point of three major ocean currents and in combination with tides and wind, these provide the most treacherous waters for small vessels working inshore. The preponderance of wreckage is found in the most dangerous waters."

Conclusions: "The findings of the divers confirm that Scatarie Island is indeed surrounded by wrecks and artifacts from wrecks, some of major historical importance. Some of the items found are said to be unique."

In the summer of 1973, David Dow, a mining engineer by trade but a passionate historian by avocation, was part of the DEVCO team investigating the possibility of setting up a scuba tourism facility for Cape Breton and he employed a team of local divers to explore and assess the project. One of the shipwreck sites they visited was the *Leonidas* or the "copper coin wreck," as it is referred to by the locals.

Alex Storm and Adrian Richards first discovered HMS *Leonidas* on September 17, 1968. The DEVCO divers brought up a handful of battered and corroded copper coins from the wreck site. After brightening them with a dip in citric acid, David Dow noted that they all bore the date 1831. There was no indication of value, but they also bore the word *Britanniar* and the name *Gulielmus*. There were three different sizes of coins. Dow wrote to the Royal Mint in London and asked if they could identify the shipment. He eventually received a reply from G.P. Dyer, Librarian and Curator at the Mint, not only identifying the shipment but enclosing photocopies of all the relevant Mint documents from which Dow was able to piece together the following unique story.

The Lost Coppers of Canada

When William IV ascended the throne in 1830, upon the death of his brother, the dissolute George IV, there was a serious shortage of currency in the various colonies of the British Empire. Canada, in particular, was in a dreadful state. London had consistently underestimated the requirements of the vigorously expanding country, with the result that Canadian businessmen accepted American, Mexican, Dutch, German, French, and even Chinese coins. Scraps of paper for as little as seven-and-a-half pence changed hands as promissory notes and business was chaotic. To the consternation of the Commissary, General Routh, stationed in Quebec, it became impossible to pay the British troops garrisoned in Canada. The outraged Routh wrote to the Royal Mint in London, demanding to be supplied with enough low value coinage so that His Majesty's soldiers could be paid properly. Routh's letter arrived just as the monarchy changed, creating immediate problems for the Mint. They had already dispensed with all the coins of the previous reign, and no new currency had yet been struck.

On July 20, 1831, Royal Mint officials prepared estimates for a "Proposed Coinage of Copper for Canada," originally calculating the profit they could make from £50,000. But conceding that "a portion of it might be returned at a loss to the Government" they then proposed a £10,000 copper penny coinage.

One Minute notes that "The halfpenny die of the new reign is quite ready, as well as the farthing. The penny die will very shortly be ready." There must have been more discussion about this "Coinage for Canada," because orders were given to proceed on July 31. On August 3 tenders were called for the supply of "thirty tons of tough copper cake" from eight suppliers. Messrs Glascott won the bid. The copper was delivered, the dies were completed and the steam powered presses of the Royal Mint clattered into production. On March 28, 1832, another Minute records that the coinage was complete.

The vast number of coins, a total of 1,930,000, was packed into 20,000 bags, which in turn were placed into 333 boxes. Two ships were chartered to carry the coins to Canada. On April 28, 1832, 163 boxes full of pennies, numbered 62 to 225, were loaded aboard HMS *Orestes*, a transport at Deptford, under the command of Captain Nicholson. The *Orestes* sailed for Halifax, Nova Scotia, and then to Quebec, apparently arriving safely with her cargo of 2,460 pounds of pennies. The rest of the pennies, together with the full consignment of halfpennies and farthings, a total of 170 boxes weighing in excess of eleven tons, were entrusted to HMS *Leonidas* on June 1, 1832.

Although the *Orestes* left England first, the *Leonidas* was the first to depart Halifax, weighing anchor on August 11. She did not get very far. Nova Scotia is a long narrow peninsula, jutting out into the Atlantic and joined to the North American continent by the isthmus of Chignecto. To get to Quebec from Halifax, a ship has to sail eastward almost 250 miles before it is able to turn north to enter the Gulf of St. Lawrence. At the eastern end of the peninsula lies Cape Breton Island, shaped like a lobster claw. Beyond that lies the infamous Scatarie Island.

Scatarie has two small useable harbours, one on the northwest side and the other on the northeast side. The eastern harbour itself contains a few tiny islands, the largest of which is Hay Island. From the southeastern tip of Hay Island, the Hell's Gate Reef runs for nearly one mile out to sea, nearly always submerged by the churning waters of the Atlantic Ocean. If you sailed in a straight line from this point, you could pass between South America and Africa, into the Antarctic, and north through the Pacific until you reached Alaska, without ever sighting land. The fetch of the Atlantic rollers, then, is incredibly large in this area. The rock formations of this coast are sedimentary in origin but have been twisted through ninety degrees in ages past. The layers of rock, sandstone alternating with shale, are now vertical, and where the sandstone has eroded away, hard, saw-toothed strips of shale lie exposed like the teeth of a gargantuan fanged mill blade. It is a fearful and dreadful coast, where an unexpected wave can sweep you off your feet, leaving you severely cut and bleeding and lucky to be alive.

Throughout the seventeenth, eighteenth and early nineteenth centuries, Cape Breton Island and most of Nova Scotia were home to a number of pirate gangs; with increased surveillance, piracy died out, only to be replaced by wrecking. Add to this the icy cold Labrador Current that runs south along the coast, so in the summer the warm damp southwesterly wind brings thick fog when it crosses the cold sea. Although Nova Scotia has roughly the same area as England and Wales, even today its population is less than one million. It was only a few thousand in 1832, and both wrecking and smuggling went undetected. Indeed, the latter continues even today.

The wreckers on Scatarie planned well. The low lying swampy tip of the island was hidden by the fog bank. The false light was on top of a hillock over one mile to the west. Everything looked normal from the ship, still blowing along with all sails set. "Land dead ahead," shouts the lookout, and the helm is put hard over. Too late! The ship runs into the terrible reef which lies just thirty feet from the shore of Hay Island. Her bottom is ripped wide open, and down to the floor of the ocean tumbles her ballast, her cargo of cannons, wrought iron work, muskets, pistols, casks of powder and shot, copper ingots, and the 170 boxes of the special Copper Coinage for Canada.

But the wreckers are not to have it all their own way. HMS *Leonidas* also carries a detachment of the 79th Regiment of Foot Soldiers under the doughty Captain Mathias. The soldiers, passengers and crew get safely ashore and all are transported to Sydney, Cape Breton, unhurt. Captain Mathias submits his expense claim; the sunken vessels rigging, sails, etc., are sold the next week for £350, and the coins lay forgotten at the bottom of the sea until 1968.

The boxes of coins from the wreck of the *Leonidas* eventually broke open, and the coins were swept to and fro in the rock basin with the tides and waves. Many were worn paper thin, others were bent double by the force of the waves, and all were badly damaged and are of little interest to serious collectors of "mint condition" coins.

Still yet another expedition visited the island shortly after the DEVCO expedition. This time the divers were from the National Geographic Society searching for what they termed "an important shipwreck from the 1500s." Probably the most recent person to take an interest in the shipwrecks of Scatarie Island was Robert Marx, a famous American author, maritime historian and marine archaeologist. He visited and dived Scatarie Island and many other parts of Cape Breton in the early 1980s. What he was searching for remains a mystery.

According to professional shipwreck researcher David Barron at Northern Maritime Research in Bedford, Nova Scotia, there are 184 recorded shipwrecks on or around Scatarie Island. The seabed around Scatarie is a mass of tangled wreckage with one vessel piled on top of another, a graveyard for dozens of cannons, cannon balls, lead shot and long brass trunnels which held naval ships' planking to the ribs. Some say, there is treasure too.

Selected Shipwrecks on Scatarie Island

Agra: Ship Registration No. 048438. This 931-ton brig wrecked on May 18, 1896, in bad weather six miles north of Louisbourg while on a voyage from Pensacola, Florida, to Sydney, Nova Scotia. She was built in 1862 and registered in Sandefjord, Norway.

Cape Breton: Ship Registration No. 097808. Wrecked March 7, 1920, at Southeast Point, the SS *Cape Breton* was built March 23, 1833, by Benjamin Wallis and Co. of Blackwell, Middlesex, U.K. The steamship had one deck, two masts, 1,109 gross tons and her dimensions were 104.6 by 20.8 by 9.8 feet. She was propelled by steam with a standing bowsprit, had a square stern and a bird figurehead. An interesting point is that the steamer made her maiden voyage across the Atlantic from England to Nova Scotia, arriving in North Sydney Harbour on August 4, 1833, loaded with supplies for the collieries of Cape Breton. If, in fact, this is so then the *Cape Breton* would be the first steamer to have actually crossed the Atlantic, rather than the *Royal William* which crossed from Nova Scotia to England, leaving August 18, 1833, fourteen days after the SS *Cape Breton* had completed her crossing.

Cienfuegos: This 1,139-ton steamship was wrecked at Marks Rocks on Scatarie Island on July 19, 1914, while on a voyage from Gulfport, Mississippi, to Montreal, Quebec, with a cargo of hard pine. Her captain was S.J. Johannessen and she was registered in Cuba.

Ciss: The cargo ship SS *Ciss* was wrecked on February 9, 1941, in the Main-a-Dieu Passage at West Point on Scatarie Island. Built at Trondheim in 1925, she was 1,159 gross tons and measured 226 by 36 by 15 feet. She was owned by a Mr. Brovig in 1935 and was equipped with triple expansion steam engines.

Fidelity: The 303-ton immigrant brigantine *Fidelity* wrecked on May 10, 1834, while on a voyage from Dublin, Ireland, to Quebec. All 157 passengers were landed safely on the island. For whatever reason, three passengers were left behind on the island. One was found nine days later but died upon arrival at Main-a-Dieu; the other two were picked up by a fisherman three weeks later.

HMS Feversham: This 36-gun, 372-ton British 5th Rate frigate was built in Shoreham, England, in 1692. Under the command of Captain Robert Paston, it wrecked on Southern Point on October 7, 1711, while on a voyage from New York to Quebec as part of Admiral Walker's fleet. Her dimensions were 107 feet long and 28 feet wide.

HMS Joseph, HMS Mary, HMS Neptune: These three British transports were wrecked on October 7, 1711, while on a voyage from New York to Quebec as part of Admiral Walker's fleet. They met their fate in a bay to the west of the HMS *Feversham* on Scatarie Island.

HMS Leonidas: This 300-ton military transport ship carrying eight tons of copper coins wrecked on Hay Island in Eastern Harbour in 1832.

HMS Roseby: This British store ship wrecked in late December 1745.

HMS Rover: This 356-ton, 14-gun sloop of war under the command of Captain George Irvine wrecked on Scatarie Island on July 23, 1798, while on a voyage from Halifax to Sydney. She was built in Bermuda in 1796 and her dimensions were 104 feet long by 26 feet wide. Because of the incident, Captain Irvine was court marshaled on August 3, 1798.

HMS Savage: This eight-gun armed sloop wrecked on September 16, 1776. She was built in 1775 and her captain was Hugh Bromelge.

Le Jeune Alexandre: This three-masted tall ship wrecked in Eastern Harbour sometime in 1732.

Madge Wildfire: The 842-ton barkantine carrying a cargo of fire hydrants on a voyage from West Hartpool, U.K., to Sydney wrecked in Tin Cove.

Saltwell: The 1,167-ton steamship SS *Saltwell* was wrecked during the Great August Gale of 1873, while on a voyage from London, U.K., to Sydney. She was built in North Shields, England, in 1872 and her home port was Newcastle, England. She was under the command of Captain Mace when she foundered at 11 p.m. Sunday night near Hay Island. Of twenty-three crew members, six were lost. It was rumoured at the time of her sinking that she had onboard a very precious cargo.

Susanah: In 1834 the 332-ton ship immigrant ship *Susanah* wrecked on Scatarie Island.

Ringhorn: The 1,790-ton Norwegian steamer *Ringhorn* was built at by Laxevagaas Maskin & Jernskibs in Bergen, Norway, in 1904. She was equipped with triple expansion engines and her dimensions were 268 by 38.8 by 17.5 feet. She was under the command of Captain Halverson on a voyage from Parrsboro, Nova Scotia, to Manchester, England, with a cargo of lumber when she wrecked at Tin Cove on August 7, 1926. Five people were lost out of a crew of sixteen.

William Law: Ship Registration No. 075758. Built in 1879 at Tusket, Nova Scotia, by James A. Hatfield, this 1,599-ton sailing ship under the command of Captain William Hibbert wrecked on May 25, 1886, at Michael's Point on the west side of the island while on a voyage to Sydney in ballast. Owned by William Law and Co., her dimensions were 220 by 40 by 24 feet.

5

Louisbourg Harbour

The Fortress of Louisbourg, built by France in 1713, stood as a symbol of French dominance in the New World until 1758, when it was captured a second and final time by British forces and totally destroyed.

The lighthouse at Louisbourg was established by the French in 1734, and was Canada's first and North America's second lighthouse (the first was the Boston Harbor Light in Massachusetts, established in 1716). During war between the French and British, the lighthouse was burned to its foundations in 1736. It was rebuilt several times, and the surviving tower was constructed in 1923-24.

Between 1713 and 1758 there are twenty-six documented shipwrecks that occurred in or near Louisbourg Harbour. Most were small fishing schooners that were blown ashore in storms. The second siege of 1758 stands out as the single greatest cause of shipwrecks. The exact number of shipwrecks that occurred during this siege is open to debate. However, it is known that the townspeople witnessed the destruction of nine vessels. Since 1960 the fortress has undergone a massive reconstruction, funded by the

Fortress Louisbourg
(Photo by Terry Dwyer)

Government of Canada through the National Historic Parks and Sites program.

In the summer of 1959 marine archaeologist J. Russell Harper led the first team to systematically survey the shipwrecks in Louisbourg Harbour. Mostly shallow water wrecks were located and mapped. During the summer of 1961 Professors Erik S. Hanson and J. Sherman Bleakney and a group of divers from Acadia University in Nova Scotia did a second survey. The Acadia team revisited the wrecks previously found and added some new channel wrecks. The group concentrated their efforts on investigating those areas reported to contain shipwrecks or shipwreck material, such as cannons. As a result the survey was successful in locating eight eighteenth-century shipwrecks. The third systematic effort was during the summer of 1962 by the Steven J. Gluckman underwater archaeology team, of which Alex Storm was a member. All previously found wrecks were revisited and mapped with some new features and wrecks added in the channel areas. It was during this survey on August 27, 1962, that the *Celebre* wreck site was found and mapped.

Since then, the Parks Canada Underwater Marine Archaeology Unit from Ottawa has conducted three more surveys of these sites. To date five sites (*Celebre, Prudent, Entreprenant, Capricieux,*

A cannon from a French naval ship sunk during the siege of 1758 is
salvaged from the bottom of Louisbourg Harbour, December 2, 1927.
(Photo from the author's collection)

and one of the channel wrecks) have been surveyed by the Unit,
three of which (*Celebre, Prudent* and one channel wreck) have
been archaeologically mapped and are open to visiting divers.

The *Celebre* was a 64-gun French warship built in 1755 in
France. It is resting in twenty feet of water in the southwest arm,
very near the fortress. Depending on what time of year you visit
the wreck, the visibility will vary from ten feet to thirty feet. The
wreck site consists of a large ballast pile, limited structure and a
variety of shipboard artifacts, extending over an area of 150 feet
by 36 feet. The most conspicuous of artifacts are the cannons.
There are thirty-three complete and four broken cannons of various calibres and they are spread out over the entire length of the
site. All are heavily corroded and although appearing quite massive and indestructible, they are in fact very fragile. The site is
also littered with cannon balls and bar shots.

The *Prudent*, a 74-gun French warship built in 1753, is in fifteen feet of water at Careening Point in the harbour. Much of
what remains of this once proud vessel is now encased in a hard
protective coral and is not as fragile as the *Celebre*. Noteworthy
is the large number of exposed floor timbers. This wreck also has
numerous blocks of shifting ballast and broken cannons.

One of the most interesting features of this wreck site is the mast step/shot locker. Here, a large mound of concreted cannon balls surrounds an open cavity where the main mast once stood. The cavity still contains remnants of the burned-out mast. The size of the mound suggests that *Prudent* had an ample supply of shot remaining when it was destroyed.

The eighteenth-century shipwrecks of Louisbourg Harbour are managed and protected by Parks Canada with the cooperation of Transport Canada. A permit, issued by the Harbour Master, is required to operate dive charters or tours inside the harbour. Dive tour operators and visiting divers must follow a number of guidelines established by Parks Canada. Any readers who have not yet had the opportunity to dive these majestic time capsules from the eighteenth century should endeavour to do so.

At the entrance of Louisbourg Harbour lie the remains of the British cargo ship *Evelyn* wrecked on January 9, 1913. She was on a voyage from Bremen, Germany, to Savannah, Georgia, with a cargo of salt. The 3,664-ton *Evelyn* was built by the Greatham Steamship Co. in 1906. She was 340 by 48.2 by 12.9 feet, equipped with triple expansion engines and was owned and operated by Irvincs S.B. & D.D. Co. The wreck site is approximately two hundred feet long and the depth varies from forty to sixty feet. Visibility will vary from twenty to sixty feet depending on what time of year you dive. Visiting divers should allow for two boat dives to thoroughly explore this site.

Just a few miles north of Louisbourg at Gooseberry Cove lies the 2,561-ton SS *Montara,* wrecked on August 13, 1920. The *Montara* was bound from Botwood, Newfoundland, en route to Louisbourg. She was built in 1881 and was 315 feet long and 39 feet wide. The deepest section of the wreck is located at a depth of sixty feet and the shallow section is located in twenty-five feet. Divers should allow for a two-tank boat dive to thoroughly explore this wreck site. Also in the same area, at the entrance to Gooseberry Cove, are the remains of the *Astraea.*

The barque *Astraea* under the command of Captain W. Ridley was bound from Limerick, Ireland, to Quebec when it wrecked on May 7, 1834, at Lorraine Head. She struck on the rocks in the middle of the night and went to pieces in a matter of hours. Out of 251 people onboard only three survived to tell the tale. Most of the steerage passengers were farmers and their families, and almost all of them drowned in a state of nudity: it was believed the habit of the lower class Irish to retire to rest without a night-dress. The residents of Little Lorraine, a fishing community just north of Louisbourg, were burdened with the task of dealing with 248 naked corpses. These local inhabitants were very careful to dress them appropriately: shirt, trousers, and jacket for the men; chemise, petticoat and dress for the women. They also insisted on burying them before sunset, to ensure the spirits of the dead would not remain above ground.

This painstaking work was undertaken by fifteen men and their families in Little Lorraine in 1834. It was a busy time, but they couldn't in good conscience leave the bodies prey to wild animals or decomposition in order to tend to the fields. Although the loss of life was not as high as in other shipwrecks, the *Astraea* was more dramatic in that it happened close to land, the corpses washing on shore as a mute reminder of the need for light-houses.

Like many others at that time, the ships were on their way from Great Britain to the New World. Unscrupulous ship owners crowded people like livestock on old decrepit ships to profit from the tide of emigration from overpopulation or religious persecu-tion in Great Britain. Many ships were navigating the treacher-ous route past Cape Breton to the St. Lawrence River. Instead of reaching a land of milk and honey, many had their possessions plundered, or were tossed into the sea, prey to an icy demise on the southeast coast of Cape Breton. It was because of four shipwrecks in the spring of 1834 and the sinking of the *Astraea* close to shore that same year that the government of Nova Scotia finally appointed a superintendent of shipwrecks for northeast and southeast Cape Breton.

The British government finally offered to erect two light-houses if Lower Canada and the three Maritime provinces would share in the financing. After 1839 a system of lighthouses was instituted along the coast of Cape Breton, and although ship-wrecks still occurred, the number of victims meeting a watery grave diminished sharply.

There are many other excellent wreck dives in this area, and many wrecks waiting to be discovered. I have only highlighted a few of the better known sites. A weekend dive trip to the scenic and historic town of Louisbourg will afford you four excellent boat dives. Make sure you explore the *Celebre* and the *Prudent*, two well-preserved shipwrecks from 1758. You will not be disappointed. Also allow a few extra hours to visit Fortress Louisbourg, where you will get the opportunity to step through a doorway in time to the year 1744.

Selected Shipwrecks along the Louisbourg Coast

Acadian: Ship Registration No. 061157. This 931-ton coal carrier was wrecked in February of 1899 near Louisbourg. She was built at Sunderland, U.K., in 1872 and her dimensions were 205 feet long by 29 feet wide.

Angola: Ship Registration No. 097875. This 2,831-ton steamship was wrecked in July 1906 near Louisbourg while on a voyage from Vera Cruz, Mexico, to Montreal. Built in 1891 by R. Dixon and Co., her dimensions were 312 by 39.2 by 24.6 feet and she was equipped with triple expansion engines. At the time of her sinking she was operated by Elder Dempster Shipping.

Callisto: The Dutch freighter *Callisto*, under command of Captain F. de Haak, left San Domingo, Cuba, on April 20, 1928, bound for Montreal with six thousand tons of sugar. On April 28, the *Callisto* wrecked near Port Nova Island in dense fog. The entire crew of thirty-two people drowned. Only one body was ever recovered by fishermen and he was buried near Main-A-Dieu. The *Callisto* was built in 1920 in Rotterdam, Holland, and was 4,310 gross tons. Her dimensions were 377.6 feet. by 51.6 beam by 25.1 depth. It was rumoured at the time that the ship's safe contained something very valuable but to date nothing has not been recovered.

Evelyn: Ship Registration No. 118893. On a voyage from Bremen, Germany, to Savannah, Georgia, with a cargo of salt, the 3,664-ton *Evelyn* wrecked on January 9, 1913. Built by Irvines S.B. & D.D. Co. in 1906, she was owned and operated by Greatham &

The Callisto and her crew were lost in April 1928 near Port Nova Island.
(Photo courtesy of Roel Zwama)

Son Steamship Co. and under the command of Captain G. Higginbotham. Her dimensions were 340 by 48.2 by 12.9 feet and she was equipped with triple expansion engines.

Mizpah: Ship Registration No. 066696. The 898-ton barque *Mizpah* wrecked at Simon's Point near Louisbourg on May 26, 1887, while on a voyage from Philadelphia to Quebec. Her port of registry was Yarmouth.

SS Montara: Ship Registration No. 080808. The SS *Montara* was bound from Botwood, Newfoundland, en route to Louisbourg when she wrecked in Gooseberry Cove on August 13, 1920. Built in 1881, Montara was 315 feet long and 39 feet wide.

SC 709: Built at North Carolina in November 1942, the 120-foot long Sub Chaser 709 was commanded by Lt. William C. French. She was on a voyage from Portland, Maine, to Argentia, Newfoundland, when she wrecked at the entrance to Louisbourg Harbour on January 21, 1943. She was equipped with one three-inch gun, two 20 mm. guns, sounding gear, radar, and submarine detection equipment. The cause of sinking was severe ice build up.

Selected Shipwrecks on the
Forchu-Framboise Coast

Afgan Prince: Ship Registration No. 118617. Launched June 26, 1903, by Short Brothers Ltd., Sunderland, U.K., Yard No. 311, for Prince Line Ltd., she was equipped with triple expansion steam engines by G. Clark Ltd., Sunderland, and her dimensions were 410.2 by 52.1 by 28.8 feet. She was wrecked July 30, 1918, on Guyon Island near Gabarus while on a voyage from Hampton Roads, Virginia, with a general cargo of steel rails. The *Afgan Prince* was 3,182 net tons and registered in Newcastle, U.K.

Atlantic: Ship Registration No. 122143. The 98-ton schooner wrecked on June 14, 1917, at Bad Neighbour Shoal near Forchu Harbour while on a voyage from Halifax to Forchu. The *Atlantic* was built in Shelburne, Nova Scotia, in 1906 by John A. McGowan, owned and operated by Tug Atlantic Ltd. Her captain was E.J. Gilbert and her dimensions were 92 by 18 by 8 feet.

Canby: Ship Registration No. 131402. Built in December 1911 by Short Brothers Ltd., Sunderland, as the *Wabana* for the British and Chilean Steamship Co. Ltd. (W. Lowden and Co. managers), the ship was equipped with triple expansion steam engines by George Clark Ltd., Sunderland. Her dimensions were 2,676 tons, 375 by 52 by 28 feet. In 1920 she was sold to Wabana Steamship Co. Ltd. (Andrew L Hamilton), London, in 1922. She was registered in Halifax, Nova Scotia, in 1927. Her management was taken over by Dominion Shipping Co. Ltd., Montreal, in 1930. In 1931 she was purchased and renamed the *Canby*, registered to the Ropner Shipping Co. Ltd. She wrecked on February 19, 1934, one mile east of Guyon Island, Cape Breton, while on a voyage from Saint John, New Brunswick, to Louisbourg.

Dufferin Bell: Formerly a steamer called the *Dufferin Park*, she wrecked in 1951.

Floriston: Ship Registration No. 110335. A steel hull freighter of 2,236 net tons, *Floriston* wrecked near Guyon Island on October 12, 1914, bound from Montreal to Avonmouth with a cargo of wheat and tobacco. The *Floriston* was launched May 26, 1899, by Ropner and Son at Stockton on the Tees (Yard No. 359) for R. Chapman and Son at a cost of £35,000. She was equipped with triple expansion steam engines by Blair and Co. Ltd., Stockton on the Tees, and her dimensions were 325 by 46 by 21 feet.

Haloodan: Wrecked near Gabarus on October 23, 1911, the *Haloodan* was 2,434 net tons. Registered in Drammen, Norway, she was travelling from Chile to Montreal.

Harriet: This sailing ship wrecked at Harriet Cove, Framboise.

Langleeridge: Ship Registration No. 148081. A British collier with a cargo of coal, wrecked May 8, 1935, at Bull Rock near Guyon Island. Formerly the *Alistruther,* she was owned by F. Carrick's Medomsley Steamship Co. Ltd. in Newcastle, U.K. Built in 1924 by Smith's Dock Co. Ltd. in Middlesbrough, U.K., her registered dimensions were 350 by 50 by 24.5 feet and she was 3,811 gross tons.

Iceland II: Ship Registration No. 319607. This 91-foot-long, 62-ton steel stern dragger wrecked in a storm on February 24, 1967, while on a voyage from Souris, P.E.I., to Forchu. There were no survivors from the crew of ten. Only one body was recovered. Her captain was Thomas Hodder.

John Harvey: Ship Registration No. 127696. This three-masted 99-ton schooner en route from Gloucester, Massachusetts, with a general cargo bound for St. Pierre wrecked at Winging Point, Gabarus, in January 1912. Her captain was George J. Kearley.

Justice H: Ship Registration No. 130593. A 48-ton, two-masted schooner, this ship wrecked in Framboise Bay, Forchu, on February 18, 1913, while on a voyage from Halifax to Forchu. She was owned by Albert B. Hooper and her dimensions were 60 by 18 by 8 feet.

La Marie Joseph: The King's ship *La Marie Joseph* left Port Dauphin (Englishtown) on St. Ann's Bay, Cape Breton, on October 9, 1719, bound for Louisbourg with a cargo of limestone, plaster and some passengers. On the 10th she encountered a heavy northwest gale and lost her main sail. On the 11th her main mast broke away. On the 12th a southeast gale with fog caused her to be cast ashore about twenty miles west of Louisbourg. The crew and passengers were saved with the exception of a sergeant's wife and child.

Mikado: Ship Registration No. 121063. The beam trawler under charter to the National Fish Company, en route from Canso to Louisbourg for bunker coal, wrecked in early May 1924 at Winging Point Rock, near Winging Point, Framboise (not to be confused with Winging Point, Gabarus, ten miles in the other direction). Of the seventeen crew members, only twelve survived.

Marshall Frank: A two-masted fishing schooner similar to the *Bluenose*, *Marshall Frank* wrecked in Marie Joseph Inlet in February 1949. Ten crew members including the captain got off; the other five crew members chose to stay on the wrecked vessel. Later that day as they were attempting to leave the ship, they perished when their dories capsized in heavy surf.

Pro Patricia: A 380-ton steamer from St. Pierre-Miquelon, she wrecked near Forchu on May 29, 1905.

Restless: Ship Registration No. 146675. The 61-ton vessel from the U.K. wrecked near Forchu Harbour on August 29, 1925.

S.P. Willard: This 127-ton fishing schooner from Gloucester, Massachusetts, commanded by Captain I.E. Burton, wrecked on Guyon Island on December 30, 1912.

Thordoc: Ship Registration No. 125442. This was an old steamer from the Great Lakes bound for Louisbourg when it wrecked at Winging Point Rock. The entire crew was saved and the *Thordoc* was eventually cut up for scrap metal. Most of it was hauled out from Winging Point to the steel plant in Sydney.

Selected Shipwrecks on the Richmond County Coast

Arrow: Built in 1948 by Bethlehem Sparrows Point Shipyard, Sparrows Point, Maryland, it was originally named the *Sea Robin*. The next owner changed the ship's name to the *Olympic Games* in 1960; its final owner, Sunstone Marine in Panama, renamed it the *Arrow* in 1962. The *Arrow* was carrying a cargo of 18,000 tons of Bunker C fuel oil when it wrecked on Cerberus Rock in Chedabucto Bay on February 4, 1970, in heavy rain and 60-knot winds. One of the worst oil spill pollution disasters to occur on this coast, it created an oil slick three miles long and a hundred

The *Arrow* wrecked on Cerberus Rock in Chedabucto Bay
February 4, 1970, resulting in one of the worst oil pollution spills on
Canada's Atlantic coast. (Photo Shipsearch Marine)

yards wide, which eventually polluted forty miles of coastline. The wreck broke in two on February 8 and the stern section sank four days later in heavy seas.

HMS Ferret: On September 24, 1757, the 28-gun HMS *Ferret*, a 255-ton ship sloop, was part of Admiral Holbourne's squadron. She is believed to have foundered near Halifax, Nova Scotia, in a hurricane. Commanded by Authur Upton, she was launched on April 10, 1743, and her dimensions were 88 feet by 25 feet.

HMS Tilbury: On September 24, 1757, the 60-gun HMS *Tilbury*, a ship of 1,124-tons, part of Admiral Holbourne's squadron, wrecked near St. Esprit, Cape Breton, in a hurricane. The bow was wrecked on shore; the main body of the wreck was discovered in 1986. The stern section, along with fifteen cannons and the bulk of treasure (eight chests of coins), was never found. The *Tilbury* was launched July 20, 1745, at Portsmouth, U.K.; her captain was Henry Barnsley and her dimensions were 147 feet by 42 feet.

La Liberte: The *La Liberte* was a French frigate, lost on December 11, 1719, off St. Esprit, carrying $500,000 in gold and silver bullion.

Le St. Michel: A 36-gun French frigate *Le St. Michel,* carrying 48,000 pieces of silver and 2,000 gold coins to pay the troops at Louisbourg, was dispatched to search for, intercept and protect the *Le Triton*. It wrecked in a hurricane along with *Le Triton* in June of 1745.

Le Triton: This 600-ton, 28-gun French East India Company treasure ship, en route to France via Louisbourg from Bengal, India, via Lima, Peru, wrecked in a hurricane in June of 1745.

6

Halifax Harbour and Approaches

Halifax, the capital of Nova Scotia, is situated on the western side of Halifax Harbour, which opens on the Atlantic Ocean. The Mi'kmaq name was *Chebookt* meaning "Chief Harbour" or "Great Long Harbour." When the French explorer Samuel de Champlain visited it in 1697 he described it as "a very safe bay, seven or eight leagues [about twenty-five miles] in circumference." When Louisbourg was restored to France in 1748, the British government agreed to the demand of New England and established an Imperial military and naval base at Chebucto as a counterpoint to the French fortress at Louisbourg. Founded by Sir Edward Cornwallis on June 21, 1749, Halifax became the major base for the British Navy in North America.

At the approaches to Halifax Harbour is Sambro Island and here the Sambro Island lighthouse stands on a granite rock about two nautical miles outside the entrance to the harbour, marking an area of dangerous shoals. The harbour, which is comprised of a wide entrance, a main harbour, a narrow channel, and a large basin almost surrounded by land, is the second largest ice-free harbour in the world. Only Sydney, Australia, is larger. Halifax offered the British a safe haven for the largest fleet they could envision. The entrance is, however, often masked in fog and the more than thirty shoals surrounding Sambro Island are considered even more of a hazard.

Built in 1758 and lit in 1760, the Sambro Island lighthouse has stood guard off Halifax for the past 244 years. It has seen vessels of both the Royal and the Canadian Navies pass in peace and war; it has greeted immigrants, war brides, and refugees to a new land; it has watched the passing of the fishing boats, great and small, and the spreading sails of the yachting fleets. For sailors, it is the last sight or sound of Halifax, or the first on a safe return. Today it is the oldest lighthouse still in operation in North America.

Halifax Harbour and Approaches is the final resting place of 250 known and documented shipwrecks. The Halifax Regional Municipality is home to the largest population of recreational, scientific, military and commercial divers in Eastern Canada, yet to date less than 25 percent of these wrecks have been actually located and visited by divers, making the potential for discovery of new shipwrecks unlimited.

One of the earliest recorded shipwrecks was the sloop *Granby*, out of Boston, in 1771, with the loss of all hands. The *Granby* was a payship carrying a large payroll to the dockyard at Halifax.

The Chronicle of December 11, 1779, reported a double wreck at the entrance to Halifax Harbour: "Last Sunday morning (11th) between one and two o'clock, H.M. Sloop of War *North* (20 [guns]) and the armed ship *St. Helena*, coming into Halifax harbor from Spanish River [Sydney] during a heavy S.E. gale, were driven on shore about one league from the light-house. By which accident both ships were unfortunately lost, and about 170 persons perished. Among the *North*'s passengers were Capt. McLean of the 84th Regt., and Lieut. Butler of the Marines. Capt. Selby and the whole ship's company, with the exception of two seamen, were lost. On the *St. Helena* were Lieut. Robertson of the transport service, and three officers of the 74th Regiment. All were saved with the exception of one seaman."

The SS Daniel Steinmann

The SS *Daniel Steinmann* was one of the worst shipwreck disasters that occurred off the coast of Nova Scotia. The captain mistook the Sambro Island light for the Chebucto Head light. At 10 p.m. on the night of April 3, 1884, the SS *Daniel Steinmann* first struck on Broad Breaker then backed on to Mad Rock Shoal very near where she sank in ninety feet of water, only a few hundred yards off Outer Sambro Island.

Her master was Captain Henri Schoonhoven, who had been at sea for twenty-four years, three on the *Daniel Steinmann,* and never before had an accident. The ship left Antwerp on March 30 bound for Halifax, with a general cargo of two thousand tons, ninety passengers (mostly German immigrants) and a crew of thirty-six men aboard. Only nine people would survive.

The *Halifax Herald* newspaper reported many stories and interviews that described tragedy, heroism and unspeakable acts of cowardice that were committed by crew members and passengers. There was a great deal of confusion on the ship after she struck. Passengers and crew alike were shouting, crying, swearing and praying.

One of the surviving crew members, Florentine Von Geissel, the man on the lookout at the time of the wreck, testified at the inquiry: "Just as we let go of the anchor the ship struck heavily amidships, all hands ran aft and many were swept off the ship by a tremendous wave. A number of people were in the lifeboats on the port side. Nobody seemed to be in the other three boats. I ran to the second boat on the port side – the jolly boat – and jumped into it with Otto Crausse, a seaman, and as the ship was sinking we cut the pulley with an axe and let her drop into the sea, quickly shoving off from the sinking ship to get away from the suction. As we were doing this a man jumped from the bridge into the boat headfirst. He was a passenger. All of this occurred within minutes.

"When the ship went down only one davit fall of the lifeboat had been cut and this lifeboat full of people, mostly sailors, went down with the ship. As she sank the boatswain, a boy (a coal trimmer) and a fireman leaped from the stern of the sinking life-boat into our boat. We then got out of the suction.

"The whole of the passengers and crew were struggling in the water. We rowed our lifeboat through a struggling mass of humanity. People were crowding around the lifeboats and it was impossible to do much. Many of them made a grab for our oars, but we beat them off. I heard people in the water calling out my name to save them. There were twelve people holding on to a spar. I kept clear of them. Had we attempted to save them, or the others who had appealed to us, they would have undoubtedly have swamped the lifeboat and we would have all been lost. In the darkness, excitement and terror, slow progress was made. We landed our lifeboat on Sambro Island."

Out of 126 people, only three of ninety passengers survived and only six of the thirty-six crew members.

The *Daniel Steinmann* was built by John Cockerill at Hobo-ken near Antwerp, Belgium, in 1875 for Smaler & Co. at a cost of one million francs. Originally built as the *Kbodive*, her name was changed when she changed owners. She was intended for the Baltic trade but made only two trips and was frozen in at Cron-stadt in the winter of 1875-76. On her return, it was concluded that she was too large to be profitably employed in that trade. She was sold in the latter part of 1876 to the White Cross Line, which was founded in 1844 by Steinmann and Ludwig, who were two of the most substantial and enterprising promoters of Atlantic transport service in Europe. Their line consisted of eight steam-ers; five of them ran between Antwerp and New York, and three ran between Antwerp and Halifax in the winter and Antwerp and Montreal in the summer. The *Daniel Steinmann* was an iron ship of 1,790 tons, a schooner-rigged brigantine, with two compound inverted steam engines capable of 183 horsepower. Her dimen-sions were 277.5 feet in overall length, 34.5 feet in breadth, and 25.4 feet in depth. She also had five ship bulkheads and two decks.

For divers the *Daniel Steinmann* is, in my opinion, one of the best wreck dives you will experience in Halifax Harbour and Approaches. Divers who would like to visit this remarkable ship-wreck should have the necessary specialty courses, equipment and diving experience. This particular wreck is considered to be an advanced deep dive and a dry suit, double tanks and a 30-cubic-foot pony bottle are highly recommended.

The water off Sambro Island tends to be very deep and very cold. Surface currents are always present and are a factor to be dealt with. Underwater visibility can vary from forty feet on a bad day to a hundred feet on a good day. The wreck itself is spread out over several hundred yards and many of its pieces are recognizable.

The most distinct part of the wreck site is the cargo pile which is fused together in a concretion; it is very impressive to see. If you look closely you will discover some of the many unique pieces that made up the cargo. There are intact pieces of stained glass, rolls of brass wire, barrel hoops, and cement preserved in the shape of the actual packing barrels. The patient and trained eye can see an occasional intact champagne bottle. There are large steel plates, lots of identifiable ship structure, huge boilers, bollards and the wreck is always teeming with marine life. It is an underwater photographer's or videographer's paradise.

The Portia

Another excellent wreck dive near Outer Sambro Island is the *Portia*. The *Portia* is resting in seventy feet of ice-cold but very clear water and it is also considered an advanced deep dive. Visibility can average thirty to forty feet on a bad day and as much as sixty to seventy feet on a good day. Much of the wreck is still visible including her boilers, various deck plates, bulkheads and bollards. The bow and mid sections are still visible, but the stern is buried in sand. The wreck was never really located by sport divers until the early 1980s, and even today there is still a lot to see and much to explore.

The *Portia* was an iron, schooner-rigged screw steamship of 732 tons. She was 220 feet long, 31 feet wide and 23 feet deep. She was built in Newcastle in June 1884 by Wigham Richardson and Co. for C.T. Browning & Co. of New York. The *Portia* was owned by the Red Cross Line, and at the time of her sinking

Doug Carmichael, the author, Suzie Watters and Gabe Carriere after
a dive on the shipwreck *Portia* near Sambro Island, Nova Scotia.
(Photo by Dave Gray)

was operated by the Newfoundland and Halifax Steamship Co.
She had been in the New York-Halifax-Newfoundland service
for many years and had done good work in both passenger and
freight traffic. The *Portia* had left New York two days before,
bound for Halifax then to St. John's, Newfoundland, with a full
list of passengers, most of whom were tourists. On July 11, 1899,
she ran up on the rocks of Big Fish Shoal near Sambro Island at
6:45 p.m. during dense fog in which it was impossible to see any
sign of land, rocks or a light. Her master was Captain Farrell of
Halifax. During his extensive career at sea, the *Portia* was his first
wreck.

Captain Farrell was Chief Officer for a number of years
and succeeded to command about five years before the wreck.
The *Portia* was carrying eighty passengers (thirty of whom were
women) and thirty crew members. Only one passenger lost his
life. Unlike the *Daniel Steinmann* disaster which occurred fifteen
years earlier and was mainly remembered for acts of confusion,

panic and cowardice on the part of its passengers and crew, the sinking of the *Portia* was very different.

The front page of the July 15, 1899, *Halifax Herald* read: "That the disaster was not attended by more serious consequences was due to the coolness and good management of the steamer's officers and the readiness with which their orders were obeyed by the large number of passengers onboard, for though the steamer lay in a perilous position on an isolated shoal, enveloped by dense fog, and none able to tell where they had struck and the danger of their surroundings necessitated the abandonment of the steamer forty minutes after she ran on the rocks, every soul onboard was placed safely in the ship's boats and all succeeded in reaching shore without the loss of a single life."

During the course of launching lifeboats and transporting passengers and crew to Inner Sambro Island, a poor little Assyrian boy named Basha seemed to have been forgotten. It was when they first did a count of survivors that his absence was discovered.

The *Portia* was also carrying a cargo consisting of 300 cases of fruit, 45 barrels of provisions, 763 barrels of flour, 75 barrels of oil, and a quantity of sundries. Beazley Brothers, a local diving and salvage company, salvaged whatever could be saved as quickly as possible. The divers also had the grisly task of recovering the body of the little boy who was asleep in his bunk when the wreck occurred.

The Havana

The *Havana* was at anchor, having just finished refloating the schooner *Alexander R.* It was Thursday night, April 26, 1906. It was a dark night and it is believed that the wind or current swung her around so that her lights were hidden from the lookout onboard the steamer *Strathcona*. At approximately 10:30 p.m. the two vessels came together with great force – the *Strathcona* striking the *Havana* square on the broadside and crushing through her as if she were matchwood. If the *Strathcona* had backed off, the *Havana* would have gone down the next minute and her crew might have perished. But she held on, the great gap was partially filled, and the *Havana* crew scrambled aboard the *Strathcona*. They only had time to do this, however, and no more, not even getting their clothes, other than the ones they stood in. In less than ten minutes, the *Havana* went to the bottom.

Captain J.A. Farquhar was later quoted as saying: "The *Havana* was insured by Lloyds and the underwriters paid me the insurance promptly. That compensated for the loss of the vessel, but there was one thing that no amount of insurance will ever replace. That was a prize sextant the Admiralty gave me for salvaging the guns from the HMS *Niobe* in 1874. I had taken it to sea with me around the world. Sometimes I feel like donning the diving helmet and going down for it, there where it lies in my chart room on the wreck of the *Havana*."

Built in Hantsport, Nova Scotia, by G.W. Churchill, the *Havana* was a wooden screw steamer of 471 tons owned by Captain J.A. Farquar. Forrestt and Son of London, England, manufactured her engine. The *Havana* was also classed in the American Record of Shipping and the Lloyds Register of Shipping 1906-1907. Her ship's registration number is 97185. She was equipped with "wrecking apparatus" onboard for salvage work.

For eighty-six years the *Havana* lay relatively intact and undisturbed in a hundred feet of water, not far from the Halterm Container Pier in Halifax Harbour. Then with the starting of the first Halifax Harbour Clean Up project, the Atlantic Geoscience Centre of the Bedford Institute of Oceanography did a complete side scan sonar survey of the harbour. While carrying out this survey, geologists Gordon Fader and Bob O'Miller made several new discoveries.

Their side scan sonar picked up several targets on the seafloor, many of which were shipwrecks. One particular target was estimated to be almost two hundred feet in length, and preliminary research indicated this could be the final resting place of the *Havana*. Another target was estimated to be a hundred feet long and research suggested it could be the *Gertrude De Costa*. But they had no way of knowing for sure what shipwrecks they were. It wasn't until divers visited the site and took underwater photographs and video, that the Maritime Museum of the Atlantic concluded these particular sites were in all probability the resting places of the *Havana* and the *Gertrude De Costa.*

In December 1992, I had the opportunity to dive both sites. The following notes were taken from the pages of my diver's log book.

Dive #1 (Possible resting place of the *Havana*): "What we found on the bottom of the Harbour resembled a large 150- to 200-foot schooner with a steam engine. The bow and forward section is in remarkable condition. A box of ammunition is present very near the bow. The wreck is littered with china plates, cups, bottles, artifacts, and coal. There is superstructure still remaining and most of the hull is still intact. Some of the decks and the wheel house have collapsed and the stern is almost completely gone. It was very near the stern section that we found and inadvertently recovered the ship's bell, with the intent of positively identifying the wreck. The bell as it turned out, had no name on it and is now 'in storage' at the Maritime Museum of the Atlantic.

"The water in this part of the harbour is quite dirty (visibility 15 feet), a strong current is present. There is a fishing net draped over part of the stern section of the wreck. The bow of the wreck is covered with a heavy growth of anemones and sponges but white paint is still visible on the hull."

In January of 1994 Jacques Whitford Environmental Ltd. hired our diving company, Deep Star, to carry out a complete survey of the *Havana* and the *Gertrude De Costa* wreck sites. Over thirty-two days, we carried out thirty-two decompression dives on the wreck sites. Decompression diving involves making a series of planned stops at specific depths for exact amounts of time. Divers use rigid mathematical formulas or dive tables that have to be followed religiously. These dive tables allow you to calculate the exact depth and times of your stops to allow for the excess nitrogen that accumulates in your bloodstream during a dive to be eliminated without complication. You can bend a lot of rules in life, but you will find that the rules of physics do not bend.

Our average bottom time was forty minutes at a hundred feet. We were able to shoot more than fifteen hours of underwater video and we took over 150 photographs of both sites. This was during January and February and it snowed heavily every day of the survey.

I can't help but remember starting each day by shoveling a foot of snow off the deck of the dive boat. We also had to contend with a surface temperature of -15° Fahrenheit and a wind chill factor of -30° Fahrenheit. This meant that when our dive team came to the surface after completing our dives, our masks froze over instantly and we had to pull them down over our heads so we could see our way back to the ladder on our dive boat. Water temperature at depth was 20° Fahrenheit.

I remember on one particular dive Bob Smith and I went down the anchor line and started our underwater video survey on the starboard side of the wreck. We had deliberately placed two spare scuba tanks, set up with two regulators each at thirty feet and another set attached to the anchor at a hundred feet just in case a situation should develop.

The *Havana* is 220 feet long, resting in a hundred feet of the darkest, coldest and dirtiest water in the Halifax Harbour shipping lanes. At one hundred feet the harbour water is an eerie dark green colour, and without a visual reference it can be hard to tell up from down when swimming in the water column. Average visibilty in the water column is fifteen to twenty feet. On the bottom everything is a dull gray colour and you can only see clearly what your light shines on. There are also other factors to consider, like old fishing nets and monofilament line. Then there is the physiology of deep water diving and what it can do to the human mind and body. For these reasons and more we thoroughly researched and planned every detail of the diving operations, or so we thought. It has been said that wars have been won and lost based on planning. Remember these words.

We started our descent and eight minutes later we were on the bottom, near the bow on the starboard side. We checked the spare tanks attached to the anchor, our own personal air supply, dive computers and camera systems and proceeded to swim the first 220 feet of the starboard side of the *Havana*. Thirty-five minutes later we were on the return path nearing the bow on the port side of the wreck when we noticed that the anchor and up line from our topside dive boat was gone. We could see the scour marks and a visible trail that was leading off in a westerly direction. This was not a good thing! We checked our air supply and our dive computer profile. We had spent forty-three minutes at one hundred feet and we would have to do twenty minutes of decompression before we could safely ascend to the surface. This ruled out a free swimming emergency ascent.

Now, let me tell you from personal experience this was not a good situation to be in. A lot of things go through your mind at this point; suffice to say that I was starting to feel somewhat religious. A choice had to be made and quickly as we were running out of air and time. We consulted our air gauges. We each had about 1,200 PSI of air in our double tanks (which is a little over a third of a full tank); we also had a 30-cubic-foot pony bottle each for emergency purposes. After assessing the situation we decided to first swim in the direction of where our anchor had dragged off. After a five minute swim, we found nothing so we switched to Plan B. We headed back to the bow of the wreck, ascended straight up above the wreck to thirty feet, trimed our buoyance and clipped ourselves together.

Between thirty feet and the surface was a strong surface current, at the time flowing south out of the harbour. It immediately grabbed us and started to whisk us out of the harbour toward open ocean. I could only hope that our topside support team realized that the anchor had drifted off the wreck and that we were decompressing in the water column and drifting out to sea.

After what seemed like an eternity, our dive computers cleared us to safely ascend to the surface. We had exhausted all the air in our double tanks and we were now breathing off our pony bottles. Our gauges showed 500 PSI when we began our ascent to the surface. To our surprise and relief our attentive dive support team was very much aware of our predicament. They had been following our surface bubbles since we left the wreck.

We had started our dive on the wreck site near the Halterm Container Pier. After drifting in the channel for twenty-five minutes, I remember seeing the lighthouse at Mauger's Beach on McNab's Island in the distance when I broke the surface. We climbed aboard the dive boat, cold and exhausted but very much alive.

Experience is a wonderful teacher and as one of my favourite dive magazines (*Dive Training*) always says, "A good diver is always learning." While we did prepare and research a thorough dive plan, we did learn some valuable lessons for future endeavours. (I like to think there are really no mistakes in life – only lessons.) We amended our deep water diving operations to include, among other things, actually tying in our anchor/up line to the wreck site and we now carry marker/recovery floats or surface maker buoys (SMBs). As a minimum standard on any dive over sixty feet we would carry a 30-cubic-foot pony bottle and on dives deeper than eighty feet we would also use twin tanks or "doubles" as well. We would also carry out workup training dives prior to any future deep water project.

These new practices/standards would save lives once again on a deep water (140 feet) bottom survey near the Bird Islands in St. Ann's Bay, Cape Breton, a year later. On that particular dive I was wearing a set of twin aluminum 80-cubic-foot tanks with a 30-cubic-foot pony bottle strapped on the back between the doubles. Halfway through the survey at 140 feet my regulator suddenly manfunctioned. I watched in horror as my air gauge went from 2,000 PSI to 500 PSI in less than a minute. I reached for my backup regulator, which was clipped to my harness and attached to the pony bottle on my back. The regulator was nowhere to be found. I could now feel my heart beating rapidly.

I began to reach and grope behind me for the regulator and was just about to dump my weight belt and make a free ascent when my dive buddy came to my rescue and located the regulator, which had become separated from the clip and hung up behind my tanks. I drew my first breath off the pony bottle and began my ascent.

It was then that things went from bad to worse. My dive buddy's drysuit inflator started to inflate and froze open, blowing air into his suit. We tried in vain to disconnect the hose from the inflator. In the end we opted to turn off his air, and using our 30-cubic-foot pony bottles, we both made a semi-controlled free ascent.

The lesson, or nugget of information, that I took home from that dive was to always mount my pony bottle in front of me, or on my side, so that I could always locate the regulator. If need be I could disconnect the entire system and hand it off to another diver.

We eventually went on to develop and learn a great deal about deep water diving preparations, techniques, protocol and special equipment. Two of the original divers involved with Deep Star in the early 1990s, Steve Crain and Albert Coffill, went on to become pioneers in the local technical diving community. (Technical diving involves the use of extensive equipment and rigorous protocols to go beyond the depths of recreational diving, which is 130 feet.) Bob Smith and James Semple went on to become scuba instructors in the local and the international recreational diving community. Commercial diver Derek King is now a captain on one of the harbour tug boats. I continued to stay involved in scuba retail and training while continuing to develop and pioneer the scuba tourism business here in Nova Scotia. All of us are still diving today. Over the past twelve years we have safely visited and surveyed many shallow and deep water wreck sites here in Nova Scotia and Newfoundland. Most recently we have been exploring wreck sites on St. Paul Island.

I want to clearly convey to you that there is no substitute for diving experience as this can only be attained by continuing your education, by diving frequently and consistently. It is imperative to seek out advanced scuba training, education, specialty courses and deep water training prior to visiting any deep water or offshore wreck sites.

The Deliverance

In the early morning of June 15, 1917, the *Deliverance* sailed out into a thick fog and a calm sea in Halifax Harbour. She was under charter to the Royal Canadian Navy for coastal patrol purposes. The harbour administration itself was still under the command of the British Navy. It was six months before the Halifax Explosion.

Owned by the Southern Cross Salvage Co., of Liverpool, N.S., the *Deliverance* was equipped for diving and salvage operations. She was under the command of Captain Brennan and towing another vessel. Those on the bridge of the patrol boat were able to see a half a mile or so through the early morning mist. The *Deliverance* was blowing one long and two short blasts of her whistle signifying that all ships should keep clear. Another whistle was heard. About half a mile out to sea *Deliverance*'s crew saw the Norwegian steamer *Regin* heading inbound. The *Regin* was blowing one blast to indicate she was steaming ahead. Seeing the danger of a collision, the captain of the patrol boat immediately ordered full speed astern, but according to the crew of the *Deliverance* the other steamer kept coming. Hampered by the cable attached to her tow, the *Deliverance* was unable to swing clear and caught the full force of the collision.

The *Regin* struck the *Deliverance* on the starboard side about twenty feet from the stern. Captain Brennan ordered full speed ahead and headed the *Deliverance* for Herring Cove, about three miles away, hoping to beach his ship in a safe haven. It seemed as though the *Deliverance* would be able to make it. However, it soon became apparent that the water was rapidly making headway, and those aboard the stricken steamer prepared to abandon ship. Within minutes, the sea claimed the *Deliverance* and she went to the bottom stern first. The time was 9:45 a.m.

For fifty-six years the *Deliverance* lay undisturbed in 120 feet of water, just a short distance from the mouth of Herring Cove. Then in 1974, a team of divers from the Parks Canada Underwater Marine Archaeology Unit came across her remains while doing an archeological study of the eighteenth-century ship *La Tribune*, wrecked in the same area. It wasn't until the early 1980s that sport divers began visiting the wreck of the *Deliverance*, and even today, mostly because of its depth, not many divers have been out to this remarkable site.

During the summer of 1992, seventy-five years after the sinking, a small group of divers prepared themselves by doing last minute checks prior to entering the water from our dive boat, for what would be a truly spectacular dive on the wreck of the *Deliverance*.

Bob Smith and I were the second dive team to go over the side. Slowly we began our descent, following the anchor line down into a blue-gray haze. At a depth of eighty feet, the wreck began to appear and take shape; at 110 feet we landed on the stern of the wreck next to a coil of old umbilical hose. Visibility on this dive was about twenty feet, so Bob turned on his dive light and led us towards the mid section of the wreck. As we made our way forward, we were amazed at the condition of the wreck.

The *Deliverance* is 110 feet long and 32 feet wide. The wreck is mostly together and intact, not being susceptible to the action of waves because of its depth. Most of her hull is buried. You can see the bow, stern and mid section, but because the super-structure has caved in, penetration into the wreck is impossible. As we passed over the boiler, where the wheelhouse and bridge once stood, we saw that all that remains is a mass of metal and wood, slowly showing signs of caving inward. The remains of the wheelhouse and bridge lie right beside the wreck. Forward of the boiler we continued our journey towards the bow. This section is covered in silt and is home to a large wolf eel curled up against a piece of the wreckage. On this dive, it was the only inhabitant we encountered. After a quick look at the bow section, it was time to return to the anchor line to begin our ascent back to the surface.

Our brief visit was limited to twenty minutes because of the depth. After a short safety stop, we surfaced in front of the bow of our dive boat. This was another memorable dive on one of Halifax Harbour's best dive sites.

The City of Vienna

Late in the afternoon on June 30, 1918, the steamer *City of Vienna* left the port of Montreal and made her way down the St. Lawrence towards the Atlantic Ocean. The ship had been pro-visionally fitted out for troop transportation service. There were just over 1,400 Canadian soldiers from different parts of Canada onboard the steamer. There was also a large cargo of bombs and other munitions onboard that were destined for the war in Europe.

The *City of Vienna* was bound for Halifax where a convoy of troop transports was being assembled. Because of wartime secrecy, the troops only had a vague idea, through rumours, where they were ultimately bound for. On Tuesday morning on July 2, 1918, at about 7 a.m. the *City of Vienna* struck on Black Rock at the entrance to Halifax Harbour very near Sambro Island in a thick fog. With the help of local fishermen, the entire crew and all 1,400 Canadian troops were safely landed in record time.

The *City of Vienna* was formerly of the Hall Line (Ellerman Group) and was originally an Austrian freighter that was built in 1914 by Workman Clark and Co. in Belfast, Ireland. She was 6,111 gross tons and measured 420 by 55.7 by 30.9 feet. She had been captured earlier during World War I.

The Gertrude De Costa

The *Gertrude De Costa* was a one-deck wooden auxiliary motor screw vessel built in the U.S. in 1912. Her gross tonnage was 109.72 tons and her length was 103 feet, breadth 23 feet and her draft was 10 feet. On her way in from the fishing grounds with a cargo of fish, she was proceeding into Halifax Harbour to reach the General Seafoods Wharf when she collided with the 214-foot steamer (freighter) *Island Connector* between Ives Knoll and Point Pleasant Park shortly after 2 a.m. on March 18, 1950. The vessels came together when the starboard bow of the *Island Connector* struck the starboard quarter of the *Gertrude De Costa* about aft of the main rigging.

The damage sustained by the *Island Connector* was slight; one plate on the starboard bow indented. The ship's bell was set over to starboard and lost. The damage to the *Gertrude De Costa* caused her to sink in less than one minute. Eleven crew members lost their lives and six survived. The approximate time of the sinking was 2:18 a.m. It was impossible to say how many of the crew were inside the body of the ship and how many were on deck when the vessel went down. The *Island Connector* picked up eight men out of the water and brought them aboard, two of them showing no signs of life when they were placed on the deck. A piece of cabin wreckage was hoisted aboard to see if there were any people trapped in it. There were none.

Sometime later a third body washed up on Mauger's Beach on McNab's Island in the harbour. Three days later a fourth body washed up. It is widely believed that the seven remaining members of the crew were trapped forward in the forecastle of the schooner. On March 28, the Navy announced that it was calling off the search for the *Gertrude De Costa;* after searching an area of four and a half square miles, they had found nothing.

It wasn't until April 25 that the wreck was found by searchers from the RCAF 102 Marine Squadron. Chief Petty Officer John Brown of the RCN made the perilous descent. The *Gertrude De Costa,* he said, was lying on her starboard side at a thirty-degree angle and it was impossible to go below deck. Treacherous currents were eddying around the slippery hull, which Brown reported was torn to bits in the after section where she was rammed by the *Island Connector.* He failed to locate any bodies.

For forty-two years the *Gertrude De Costa* lay undisturbed in ninety feet of water near the main shipping lane between the Ives Knoll buoy and Point Pleasant Park in Halifax Harbour. During the Halifax Harbour Clean Up Survey in December 1992 I had the opportunity to dive on this remakable shipwreck.

We landed very near the bow of what appeared to be a two-masted schooner lying on her port side. There was machinery and a lot of debris crowded around the bow and mid section. However, the bow, forecastle and hull were remarkably (75 percent) intact. The stern was completely gone and all that remained was the ship's wheel in a debris field. The engine, shaft and propeller is quite visible. The wreck is littered with rubber boots and various other personal artifacts. This served as a haunting reminder that there might still be people aboard the ship. This particular dive was probably the most eerie dive I have ever done. A combination of ice-cold, murky green water, a strong two knot current and poor visibility made for an unnerving dive. We noted that black paint was still visible on the hull. We estimated the length of the vessel to be between seventy-five and a hundred feet.

In January 1993, the CBC *Evening Edition News* aired a story about our dive on the *Gertrude De Costa* on TV, complete with never before seen underwater video footage of the wreck. The response they received was phenomenal. Relatives of the crew who died on the wreck wrote to CBC and even contacted us, wanting to share even more information about the wreck. For some of the relatives, many of whom had never known what happened to the *Gertrude De Costa* and her crew forty-three years ago on that fateful night of March 18, 1950, they could finally put to rest the memories of loved ones and a sad chapter in their lives was finally closed. Some of the relatives told me that they were never told what really happened on that night, and none of them ever received any form of compensation from the Sweeny Fishing Company of Yarmouth who owned the schooner. One woman told me about the day she first saw the *Gertrude De Costa*, tied up at the wharf in Canso: "She was painted all black and she had an eerie look about her, and the Sweeny Company was having a difficult time trying to find a crew to sail on her. I had a bad feeling about that schooner."

Selected Shipwrecks of Halifax Harbour and Approaches

A.W. Perry: Ship Registration No. 106075. The Canadian freighter *A.W. Perry* was wrecked on June 8, 1915, at Chebucto Head while on a voyage from Boston to Halifax with a general cargo. The 1,601-ton ship was built by Workman Clark and Co. in 1897. Her dimensions were 255 by 34 by 22 feet. She was operated by the Canada Atlantic & Steamship Co. and equipped with triple expansion engines.

Bohemian: Ship Registration No. 113400. The 8,555-ton *Bohemian* carrying a general cargo from Boston to Liverpool, U.K., struck on Sambro ledges in a snowstorm around three in the morning on March 1, 1920. The *Bohemian*, owned by F. Leyland and Co., was built by A. Stephen and Sons in 1900. She was equipped with triple expansion engines and her dimensions were 512 by 58.2 by 34.3 feet.

City of Brunswick: Ship Registration No. 221007. The 7,225-ton American steamer *City of Brunswick* was on a voyage from New Orleans to Antwerp, Belgium, with grain and lumber when it wrecked on Sambro Island on August 26, 1921. Built in 1921 by O. Daniels Co. and operated by the U.S. Shipping Board, she was equipped with triple expansion engines and her dimensions were 402.1 by 54 by 43.4 feet.

City of Sydney: Ship Registration No. 115274. The 2,568-ton Canadian ship *City of Sydney* wrecked on Sambro Island March 17, 1914, while on a voyage from New York to St. John's, Newfoundland. She was built in 1890 by C.S. Swan and Hunter and operated by the St. Lawrence Shipping Co. She was equipped with triple expansion engines and her dimensions were 300.4 by 41.1 by 21.6 feet.

City of Vienna: Ship Registration No. 135577. The 6,111-ton *City of Vienna* formerly of the Hall Line (Ellerman Group), was originally an Austrian freighter built in 1914 by Workman Clark and Co. in Belfast, Ireland. Her dimensions were 420 by 55.7 by 30.9 feet. She had been captured earlier during World War I.

Clare Lilly: Built in 1917 as the *Cliffside* and later renamed the *Modig* before becoming the *Clare Lilly* in 1934, she wrecked off Black Point near Portuguese Cove in Halifax Harbour on March 22, 1942. At the time of the sinking the *Clare Lilly* was carrying a cargo of bombs and munitions.

Costa Rican Trader: Ship Registration No. 1327. Formerly the *Washington Trader*, the *Ponce* and the *Mexican Trader*, this vessel was built by Union Diesel Engine Co. and the Albina Engineering and Machine Works in Poland. She was owned and operated by the Mexican Trader Corp. out of Monrovia and flew a Liberian flag. She wrecked near Herring Cove in Halifax Harbour in 1967. Her dimensions were 376.6 by 51.7 by 21.8 feet; she was 4,141 gross tons.

Damara: Ship Registration No. 090009. The 1,779-ton British cargo ship *Damara* was wrecked off Musquodoboit Harbour on February 7, 1905, while on a voyage to Halifax with a general cargo. The *Damara* was built by A. Stephens and Sons in 1885, operated by Furness, Withy and Co. and her dimensions were 275 by 35 by 15.4 feet.

Daniel Steinmann: The 1,790-ton SS *Daniel Steinmann* was on a voyage from Antwerp to Halifax when it wrecked near Sambro Island on April 3, 1884. She was built in 1875 by Societe Cockerill, operated by the White Cross Line and her dimensions were 277.5 by 34.5 by 25.4 feet.

Humboldt: The 2,190-ton *Humboldt* was one of two paddle steamers owned by the New York and Le Havre Steamship Co. and sailed under the American flag. After a very brief career of two years she was wrecked at Portuguese Cove near the entrance to Halifax Harbour on December 5, 1853. Her loss was due to a local fisherman who represented himself as an experienced pilot, although he knew little about such matters. Eight months later the other ship of the line, which had maintained the service, the *Franklin*, was wrecked off New York. Fortunately, everyone aboard the *Humboldt*, with the exception of one person, was saved. The company never recovered from the loss of these two ships and was closed in 1861, on the outbreak of the American Civil War. The *Humboldt* was built in 1851 by Westervelt and McKay of New York and her dimensions were 292 by 40 by 27 feet.

Isleworth: Ship Registration No. 132272. The 4,879-ton British cargo ship *Isleworth* wrecked at Chebucto Head at the entrance to Halifax Harbour on March 13, 1912. She was on a voyage in ballast from Boston to Halifax and then Louisbourg. The *Isleworth* was built in 1911 by Ropner and Sons, owned and operated by Watts, Watts and Co., and her dimensions were 390 by 52 by 27.8 feet.

Kenkerry: Ship Registration No. 149422. The 3,930-ton British cargo ship *Kenkerry* wrecked at Black Rock Point near Portuguese Cove on January 17, 1935, on a voyage in ballast from Havana to Halifax. The master, Captain Duncan Milne was lost. The *Kenkerry* was built in 1927 by Tyne Iron S.B. Co., operated by the Guardian Line and her dimensions were 355.3 by 50.5 by 24.1 feet.

Kolkhosnik: Ship Registration No. 139915. This Russian ship was formerly the *Rockcliffe* and was renamed the *Kolkhosnik* in 1935. While on a voyage from Boston to Halifax with a cargo of

A converted passenger line, the *Letitia* was a hospital ship during World War I. Because of pilot error, she grounded near Portuguese Cove at the entrance to Halifax Harbour on August 1, 1917. Of the 767 people onboard, only one was lost. (Photo: Shipsearch Marine)

war materials, she struck on Smithson Rock near outer Sambro Island on January 16, 1942 and sank.

La Tribune: She was wrecked in December, 1797 at the entrance to Herring Cove in Halifax Harbour. Formerly a French 44 gun frigate, she was captured by the British ship HMS *Unicorn* on June 8, 1796. She drifted ashore during a violent storm.

Letitia: Ship Registration No. 133033. Built in 1912 by Scotts Shipbuilding & Engineering Co. Ltd. in Greenock, U.K., the *Letitia* was 470 feet long and 56 feet wide; she was equipped with two triple expansion three-cylinder steam engines. The ship was operated jointly by Donaldson Brothers Ltd. and the Anchor Line (Henderson Brothers Ltd.). A converted passenger liner, the *Letitia* was operating as a hospital ship during the World War I. She was on passage from Liverpool, U.K., to Halifax, with 546 patients, 84 medical staff and 137 crew, all of whom were saved except for one crew member. The *Letitia* went aground on August 1, 1917, as a result of a pilot error near Portuguese Cove, just inside Chebucto Head at the entrance to Halifax Harbour.

Martin Van Buren: Ship Registration No. 244916. This Liberty Ship loaded with a general cargo which included locomotives and trucks was torpedoed by a German U-Boat on January 14,

1944. She drifted over five miles from where she was originally abandoned by her crew and grounded on a shoal called the Lobster Claw, near Sandy Cove in Sambro.

Salerno: Formerly *Chicago* and *Lincoln City*, the 2,672-ton iron screw steamer was built in March, 1884, by T. Richardson and Sons and W. Gray and Co. in Hartpool, U.K. Her dimensions were 301 by 40 by 22 feet and her port of registry was Tonsberg, Norway. Her Master was Captain E. Olsen and her owner was a W. Wilhelmsen.

Spyros: The Greek steamship *Spyros* carrying wheat on a voyage from Saint John, New Brunswick, to Liverpool, England, struck a rock, broke in two and sank on February 17, 1942, about twenty miles from Halifax.

7

Cape Sable and Seal Island

It is said that one of the worst places in the world is Cape Sable, the most southerly point of Nova Scotia. Cape Sable Island is the turning point for ships entering the Bay of Fundy from the east. The island is located on the west side of Barrington Bay at the south end of Nova Scotia. The Mi'kmaq name was *Kespoogwitk*, which means land's end. The Cape area was called Beusablom, which means sandy bay, as early as 1554 by Portuguese cartographers. Possibly the French explorers De Monts and Champlain used that name in the French version, Cap de Sable and Baie de Sable. The New England Planters came in 1761 and occupied the land at what the British government called Cape Sable.

The *Bridgewater Bulletin* on December 5, 1911, reported: "The dangers of Cape Shore are invested in the dangerous ledges which under run the sea at various places in the vicinity and dropping precipitously into deep water give the mariner no chance of telling his proximity by means of the lead. The whole of the southern coast of Nova Scotia is fringed with these ledges, many of them rising just shoal enough to cause breakers only during mean tides or in heavy gales. Thus, a vessel approaching their vicinity in fog or a dark night with heavy rain or snow, and keeping the lead going may get 16 fathoms [96 feet] at one sounding, and a few minutes later strikes a ledge with only 14 feet of water on it.

"If it is blowing hard and there is any sea running, she will pound to pieces very quickly, or back off and founder in deep water. The terrors of the ledges around Cape Sable are very much magnified by reason of the currents and rips caused by the tides sweeping up and down the Bay of Fundy, and the two perils combined have helped for considerably over a century to make Cape Sable and its environs a place to be dreaded by navigators. Fog is almost a permanent institution around this part of Nova Scotia, and the Cape, being in close proximity to the Gulf Stream, is within the zone of the furious storms which every now and again whirl out from that mighty current. Like Sable Island, the number of wrecks and disasters to shipping around the Cape will never be accurately known as, with the terrific seas breaking over the ledges in winter gales, the vessel striking, founders or goes to pieces immediately, while the chances for crews and passengers in the life-boats are small. Those who have survived the buffetings of the pounding breakers and the whirling tide-rips are never likely to forget them, and will always retain a shuddering memory of the terrors of Cape Sable as a lee-shore. All the ledges and rocks within a 40-mile radius of the Cape are responsible for the wreck of many a fine ship. Seal Island, Gannet Rock, Blonde Rock, Soldiers, Old Man, Tusket, Shag, and Mud Island Ledges have each exacted a heavy toll of vessels and lives."

On February 8, 1860, the 2,190-ton steamship *Hungarian* left Liverpool, U.K., for Portland, Maine. She carried 205 people and the mail. On the morning of the 20th, at about four, residents of Cape Sable Island saw her lights. At daybreak no trace of the ship could be discovered, but later six mail bags floated ashore. When the tide ebbed the ship became visible, lying in about twenty-five feet of water, her starboard bow being clear and the hull having a heavy list. One boat in good condition was found and fragments of others drifted ashore. There were also many bodies, but no survivors. An inquiry established that the lighthouse keepers at Barrington, on the mainland of Nova Scotia, had been derelict in

The Castilian on Gannet Rock Ledge, May 1899. For a few days
there were frequent sightseeing trips by tugboats to the wreck.
(Photo: Ship Search Marine)

their duty – on the night of the wreck, the light was not burning.
The *Hungarian* was built in 1859 by W. Denny and Bros., owned
and operated by the Allan Line and her dimensions were 298 by
38.5 by 17 feet.

The 7,441-ton British cargo ship *Castilian* foundered in March
1899 on the Gannet Rock Ledge about ten miles southwest of
Yarmouth, N.S., while on a voyage from Portland, Maine, to Liverpool. She was built in 1898 by Workman Clark and Co. and
operated by the Allan Line Steamship Co. and her dimensions
were 470 by 53.7 by 25.2 feet.

The first light tower built at Cape Sable was made of wood
in 1861, close to the southern seawall. On November 12 the first
lightkeeper, John Hervey Doane, lit the lamps atop the 65-foot
octagonal tower. Because more lives and property had been lost at
Cape Sable than on any other part of the coast, the installation of
a white light of the first order was recommended. However, the
decision was made to provide a red light on the cape. This red
light, with nineteen lamps, was by far the most expensive to operate of any on the coast. On a clear night, it could not be seen
over a distance of eight miles. Four-sevenths of the power of the
light was lost through the thick red glazing of the lantern.

In 1869, the lantern glazing was changed to clear with ruby
chimneys on the lamps to show a red light. This greatly improved

the range. Recommendations were made to have two lighthouses on Cape Sable, both showing a white light. In 1870 a clockwork mechanism was installed and the light was changed to flashing white. These would not only serve to distinguish this point from any other on the South Shore, but they could be arrayed so as to guide the mariner clear of the dangerous shoals lying to the west of Cape Sable.

A fog alarm building and steam-whistle came in 1876. In 1897 a sixteen-foot lifeboat was placed at Cape Sable. Lightkeeper Isaac Doane was coxswain, but he had no organized crew. In 1900, this was abandoned in favour of a new lifeboat stationed at Clark's Harbour, on Cape Sable Island.

On its low land-base, the light was not visible far enough to seaward. In 1923-24 a new tower of reinforced concrete, 101 feet from base to vane, was constructed nearby, making it the tallest lighthouse in Nova Scotia. On May 26, 1986, the Cape Sable Light was automated.

Seal Island

Seal Island lies off the southwest tip of Nova Scotia at "the elbow of the Bay of Fundy" where the broad mouth of the bay meets the open Atlantic Ocean. For more than three centuries storms, fog and powerful tides have conspired to wreck scores of ships on the island and its surrounding ledges. Seal Island is historically one of Atlantic Canada's most dangerous areas for shipping, along with Sable and St. Paul Islands.

Seal Island received its name from Samuel de Champlain when he landed there amongst the hundreds of seals in 1604; he dubbed the hazardous rocks at Seal Island the Sea Wolves. It is also the site of Nova Scotia's second oldest surviving wooden lighthouse, the Seal Island Light (established in 1831). The light was built largely through the efforts of a woman named Mary Hichens, who grew up with the tragedies of shipwrecks and even tended to the occasional survivor. The island is located eighteen miles from Clark's Harbour on Cape Sable Island in Yarmouth

County. It is roughly three miles long and one and a half miles wide.

Before anyone lived on Seal Island, shipwrecked mariners lucky enough to have reached its shores alive often died of starvation and exposure during the harsh winter months. By the early years of the nineteenth century a grim spring tradition had evolved, as preachers and residents of Yarmouth and Barrington came to the island to find and bury the dead. There was much concern about the loss of life and on one occasion twenty-one people were buried in shallow graves in one day.

The island was first settled in 1823 by two families, the Hichens and Crowells, in hopes of assisting the unfortunate souls cast ashore during the winter storms. Richard Hichens himself had been shipwrecked on Cape Sable in 1817 and later married Mary Crowell, who heard firsthand the many stories of the deaths on Seal Island from her father, a Barrington preacher. Mary Hichens, not content with the work she, her husband and his cousin's family were doing in saving lives of shipwrecked sailors, campaigned for a lighthouse to be built to warn ships of the dangers of Blonde Rock and other shoals near by. They used their own money earned from fishing and had a lifeboat built to their own design to meet the island's rugged requirements. The effectiveness of their boat was broadcast far and wide, so much so that the Royal Humane Society of England, in appreciation for their efforts, sent a set of seven life preservers to the island. The Hichens family was credited with establishing the first lifesaving station in Canada.

After several attempts to convince the Canadian government that a lighthouse was necessary, Mary Hichens eventually persuaded Sir James Kempt, Governor of Nova Scotia, to spend some time on the island. He was convinced that a lighthouse was necessary and he even surveyed for a suitable location. The highest point on the island bears his name, but the lighthouse was eventually erected nearer the shore. The House of Assembly voted £1,000 to build the structure with New Brunswick paying half the cost, as vessels bound in and out of the Bay of Fundy would benefit. Building of the first lighthouse began in 1829 and was completed in November of 1831.

Captain Hichens and Edmund Crowell alternated in keeping the light, six months at a time, and were paid £30 a year by the Canadian government. Out of this sum, they bought or built boats for rescue work and for their own business of fishing. After Captain Hichens returned to sea, Crowell took over complete supervision until his son replaced him, who in turn was succeeded by his son. When the third Crowell died his brother John kept the light for twenty-six years and was succeeded by his son-in-law Ellsworth Hamilton, who was keeper of the light for sixteen years. Then for the first time someone not related to the Hichens-Crowell family took over the lighthouse-keeping duties.

The first of what would be many recorded shipwrecks off the west side of the island at Devil's Limb was the *Adriann,* which struck the ledge in 1863.

Cunard's Royal Mail Ship *Columbia*, bound from Boston to Liverpool, U.K., via Halifax with mail and ninety passengers, wrecked on Black Ledge in thick fog on July 1, 1843. Thanks to the quick action of the islanders, all the passengers and crew were saved.

The RMS *Columbia* was one of the four original ships with which Samuel Cunard commenced his famous line in 1840, the others being the *Acadia*, the *Britannia*, and the *Caledonia*. In company with George Burns of Glasgow and David MacIver of Liverpool, Cunard entered into an agreement with the British government to run a mail steamship service between Liverpool, Halifax and Boston in return for an annual subsidy of £81,000. The service was to be every two weeks in the summer and monthly in the winter. This line was at first known as the British and North American Royal Mail Steam Packet Company, a cumbersome title which was soon dropped in favour of the simpler Cunard Steamship Company.

The signing of this contract began a regular transatlantic service, carried on by many companies on both continents, which came to be known as the "Atlantic Ferry." The RMS *Columbia* was the first casualty to be suffered by the new line. There was no loss of life and all the mail and a large part of the passengers' personal luggage was brought ashore.

Four years later the *William Abrams*, a full-rigged ship of 706 tons bound from Boston to Calcutta, struck Black Ledge. The captain, James Hamlin, first knew where he was when he discovered the wreckage of the *Columbia* nearby. Black Ledge is two miles off shore and just beyond that is Blonde Rock, which received its name from the captain of the HMS *Blonde*, a 32-gun frigate wrecked there in 1782.

The Wreck of HMS Blonde

The British man-of-war HMS *Blonde* was sent to protect the Bay of Fundy and the coast of Nova Scotia from American privateers. The HMS *Blonde* was also one of the most active privateers along the Nova Scotia coast in the years following the Declaration of Independence. She was also used as a convoy ship for British merchants and because of her size, weight and thirty-two 12-pound cannons, she was a match for any ship that tried to get too close to English merchant ships.

In early May 1782, HMS *Blonde* captured the American ship *Lyon*, a smaller vessel that was on a voyage from Beverley, Massachusetts, to Cadiz, Spain, with a load of masts and spars. Captain Tuck and his crew were taken prisoner and placed aboard the *Blonde*. The *Lyon* was sent ahead to Halifax with a British crew, as Halifax was the British Naval headquarters on this side of the Atlantic.

On May 10, 1782, while en route to Halifax in dense fog HMS *Blonde* struck an uncharted rock three and a half miles southeast of Seal Island, and sank at the spot that would forever bear her name, Blonde Rock. By means of a makeshift raft and lifeboats the British crew and their prisoners landed safely on the southwest side of the island at a place called Brig Rock. To their surprise when the fog cleared they saw that two American privateers had dropped anchor in the cove on the east side of the island: the *Lively* under the command of Captain Noah Daniel Adams and the *Scammell* commanded by Captain Noah Stoddard of Boston. The privateers had discovered an abundant supply of fire wood and fresh water and had anchored here frequently. The privateers soon found the crew from the *Lyon* and about 150 British officers and crew.

After some bargaining an agreement was reached. Captain Thornborough of HMS *Blonde* released Captain Tuck and his American crew of sixty, and provided them with a letter of safe conduct to Salem, Massachusetts, while Captain Adams of the *Lively* agreed to take the British crew off Seal Island and put them ashore somewhere near Yarmouth.

But the wreck of HMS *Blonde* and the capture of her crew did not end there. The crew found passage to Halifax aboard a small Nova Scotia privateer called the *Observer*. As they were approaching Halifax Harbour they were overtaken by the American privateer *Jack*, out of Salem and under the command of Captain Ropes. One can just imagine the surprise that Captain Ropes and his crew got when they tried to board the *Observer* and discovered over 173 well-trained British soldiers. After several hours of battle the British crew boarded the *Jack*, took her as a prize and sailed into Halifax Harbour.

The *Assaye* struck Blonde Rock on April 4, 1897. The *Assaye* was a 3,901-ton steamer, under the command of Captain I. Caruthers; she was built in Belfast and owned and operated by the English Ellman Line.

The *Assaye* left Liverpool, England, March 23, 1897, bound for Saint John, New Brunswick, with a cargo of dry goods that included, among other things, such Queen Victoria Diamond Jubilee items as engraved cutlery sets and other specially embossed items. Thanks to the Hichens family, all sixty-three crew members reached shore safely. There are approximately seventeen known ships wrecked on Blonde Rock.

The Wreck of the Staffordshire

Built in East Boston, Massachusetts, in 1851 by Donald McKay for Enock Train & Co.'s White Diamond Line, the three-masted and three-decked *Staffordshire* was one of the few clippers built for transatlantic packet service. At 1,817-tons she was 243 feet in length, 41 feet wide and had a depth of 19 feet.

On her first run in May 1851, she sailed from Boston to Liverpool, U.K., in fourteen days. In August of that year Train hired veteran clipper master Josiah Richardson to take *Staffordshire* to San Francisco, which he did in a brisk 103 days. From there they sailed to Singapore in fifty-one days, to Calcutta in twenty-one days and then to Boston in the record time of eighty-four days, a pace that few sailing ships ever bettered. Upon her return, she re-entered the Boston-Liverpool run.

The *Staffordshire's* last voyage began at Liverpool on December 9, 1853, from where she departed with 225 persons, of whom 198 were passengers, most of them Irish emigrants. On December 24 the steering gear was disabled and the bowsprit and foremast were carried away. In the course of repairs, Captain Richardson broke his ankle and injured his spine. The command of the ship then fell to the First Officer, Joseph Alden, who managed to work the vessel until January 2, 1854, when the wind moderated. On this night she ran into a snow storm. At 11:40 p.m., with the Second Officer in charge, the *Staffordshire* struck Blonde Rock off Seal Island and sank quickly, bow first. Captain Richardson gave his orders from his cabin and refused to be saved. Because there was not enough room in the lifeboats to accommodate the passengers and crew, 175 people were drowned, including Captain Richardson.

Only three lifeboats were able to get away from the wreck. One lifeboat landed at Fish Island, just inside Cape Sable, one landed at West Head on Cape Sable Island, and the third boat with seven people onboard landed at Shelburne, thirty miles up the coast. Along with the passengers and crew, the *Stafforshire* had been carrying a mixed cargo that included gold.

Rumours persisted that there was a lot of gold aboard for some purpose and the purser's safe contained a wealth of valuables belonging to the passengers. The following spring, a vessel's crew fishing in the bay saw what they thought was the hull of the *Staffordshire*, but it was too foggy to make a fix of the position from points of land and they were unable to find the spot again. During that summer a Captain Mores arrived from Boston with a diving outfit to make a thorough search for the wreck and the gold. He searched for two months but returned to Boston empty-handed.

Records kept by Richard Hichens and others over the years document 187 shipwrecks on and around Seal Island.

My first visit to Seal Island was in June of 1994 and it was an unforgettable experience. I was doing some independent free-lance work, searching for and shooting underwater video of ship-wrecks for a Nova Scotia Museum project called Operation Wreck Find and a TV series pilot project called *Oceans of Mystery*. The plan called for me and several other divers to meet at a desig-nated wharf in Clark's Harbour, near Yarmouth. There we would meet Doug Symonds and his wife Dora, who would take us out to Seal Island aboard his boat, the *Devil's Limb*, for the weekend.

So there I was, at the designated time and place at 5 a.m. Saturday morning unloading my van after a three-hour journey from Halifax. By 5:30 none of the other divers had shown up, so I located the nearest payphone and started to make calls. As it turned out none of them would be coming. Unfortunately, the weather report called for heavy fog and rough weather; as a result, the other divers canceled at the very last minute. The weather report, though, turned out to be wrong. Symonds and his wife were heading out to their cabin on Seal Island for the weekend, and he pointed out that I was still welcome to come along. We cast off the lines at 5:45 a.m. It was pitch black as we steamed out of the harbour and headed for our destination, Seal Island.

The trip would take just under three hours and already I was beginning to wonder if I should be diving alone so far offshore. We arrived around 8:30 a.m. on the south side of the island. We moored the boat and went ashore to the Symonds' cabin, where we deposited Dora and lots of supplies. The cabin was full of shipwreck memorabilia, including actual artifacts and lots of old photographs.

Now it was time to go diving. My first choice was to dive Blonde Rock, my second choice was Devil's Limb, and my third choice was anywhere else Doug could put me that he felt would contain evidence of shipwrecks. Doug pointed out that the best time to dive Blonde Rock was at slack tide and he timed it perfectly. Again he cautioned me about diving alone and strongly suggested that I not go. Nonsense, I said, I've travelled this far, so let's do it.

We headed west for about thirty minutes into a fog bank then Doug stopped the boat, pointed out off the starboard side and said, "Watch this." All I could see through the morning haze was calm, flat water, not a ripple nor a wave. As I stood there half-dressed in my diving gear and holding an underwater video system, about thirty yards from the boat the water started to boil. It was more like a pot boiling over and it kept boiling over for several minutes. Then just as quick as it started, it stopped and there sticking up out of the ocean was a rock, Blonde Rock. I captured the entire process on video. Shortly after that, several seals appeared. They were very big elephant seals (the size of my 1990 Cavalier station wagon came to mind). One of them made its way over to our boat and I watched in utter amazement as it swam right up the stern of our boat, bit a rung right off our dive ladder and swam away with it.

I began to have visions of tomorrow's newspaper headlines: *Diver attacked by monster seal. Search to resume today*. A local fisherman interviewed stated, "*I told that young fella not to go in the water*." After much careful consideration and a thorough assessment of the immediate situation, which took all of one minute not to mention there were ten to fifteen large elephant seals present, I decided it best not to enter the water at that particular time.

I began to undress and Doug turned the boat around and we headed for Devil's Limb. Upon reaching our next destination we were truly fogged in and at best we could see ten to fifteen feet around us. We headed back to our base camp, the Symonds' cabin for a cup of tea and some lunch.

By early afternoon it was apparent that the only diving I would be able to do was very near shore and under the watchful eye of Doug Symonds. I completed two separate dives that afternoon, one at Crowell Cove and one on the east side near the old breakwater. I found and videotaped lots of wreckage, including bits and pieces of boilers and engines.

The fog and the unpredictable weather had forced our hand and since I was diving alone it was best not to take any chances. I would simply have to return to this mysterious island another time, and less than a month later I returned with two other divers, Bob Smith and Steve Tower. Doug's son John Symonds and local commercial diver Donnie Mahanie took us on a day trip to a place called The Salvages. The water was gin clear and there was indeed lots of evidence of wrecks and wreckage.

Selected Shipwrecks of
Yarmouth, Shelburne and Queens Counties

Aberdeen: Ship Registration No. 103227. The 674-ton *Aberdeen* was employed as a lighthouse supply ship when she was wrecked on Black Ledge, Seal Island, October 13, 1923. She was built by Fleming and Ferguson in 1894. Her dimensions were 184 by 31.1 by 18.2 feet and she was equipped with triple expansion engines.

Assaye: The 5,129-ton steamship *Assaye* was wrecked in April 1897, on Blonde Rock south of Seal Island while on a voyage from Liverpool, England, to Saint John, New Brunswick. She was built in 1891 by Harland and Wolff and operated by Elder, Dempster and Co. Her dimensions were 401 by 45.3 by 28.1 feet.

Ben Earn: Ship Registration No. 129466. The 3,911-ton British cargo ship *Ben Earn* was wrecked on June 16, 1911, near Bacarro Point, Nova Scotia, while on a voyage from Sydney to Saint John, N.B., with a cargo of coal. She was built in 1909 by A. MacMillan and Sons, owned and operated by Straightback Steamship Co., equipped with triple expansion engines and her dimensions were 318.4 by 49.3 by 21.7 feet.

Bonavista: Ship Registration No. 087966. This 1,306-ton British iron cargo ship was wrecked on March 16, 1912, at Bear Cove, Brier Island. She was on a voyage from Saint John to Louisbourg in ballast. She was built in 1884 by Wigham Richardson and Co. and her dimensions were 240.4 by 33.5 by 18.3 feet. She was owned and operated by the Dominion Coal Co.

Brantford City: The 2,371-ton British cargo ship *Brantford City* was wrecked on August 10, 1883, near Little Harbour, Lockeport, NS, while on a voyage from London to Halifax to Boston. She was built in 1880 by W. Gray and Co., owned and operated by the Christopher Furness Line, equipped with compound inverted engines and her dimensions were 280 by 39.1 by 23 feet.

Castilian: The 7,441-ton British cargo ship *Castilian* foundered in March 1899, on the Gannet Rock Ledge about ten miles southwest of Yarmouth, while on a voyage from Portland, Maine, to Liverpool. She was built in 1898 by Workman Clark and Co. and operated by the Allan Line Steamship Co. and her dimensions were 470 by 53.7 by 25.2 feet.

Columbia: The RMS *Columbia* was one of the four original ships with which Samuel Cunard commenced his famous line in 1840, the others being the *Acadia*, the *Britannia*, and the *Caledonia*. The first casualty to be suffered by the new line was the RMS *Columbia* which wrecked in thick fog on July 1, 1843. There was no loss of life and all the mail and a large part of the passengers' personal luggage was brought ashore.

Drumalis: The 2,450-ton *Drumalis* wrecked on the Southwest Ledge near Cape Sable on August 10, 1899, while en route from Dunkirk, France, to New York.

Gerona: The 2,035-ton steamship *Gerona* struck the wreckage of the *Assaye* near Blonde Rock and foundered on December 31, 1897. The *Gerona* was on a voyage from Portland, Maine, to London, England, carrying a cargo of livestock and produce.

Etolia: The 3,220-ton British cargo ship *Etolia* was wrecked on June 9, 1906, at Cape Sable while on a voyage from Saint John, N.B., to Barrow, England, with a cargo of wood. She was built in 1887 by Harland and Wolff, operated by the Elder, Dempster Line, equipped with triple expansion engines and her dimensions were 345.6 by 40.9 by 26.7 feet.

Harlyn: The 1,453-ton British cargo ship *Harlyn* was wrecked at Cape Negro, N.S., on July 16, 1906, while on a voyage to Gloucester, Massachusetts, carrying a cargo of salt. She was built in 1891 by Edwards S.B. Co., equipped with triple expansion engines, and operated by the West Hartlepool S.N. Co. Her dimensions were 245 by 34 by 16.2 feet.

Hesper: The 2,720-ton British cargo ship *Hesper* was wrecked on Emulous Breakers, south of Ragged Island, Lockeport, N.S., on July 6, 1896, while on a voyage in ballast from Las Palmas to Saint John, N.B. She was built in 1890 by Ropner and Son, operated by George Horsely and Son, equipped with triple expansion engines and her dimensions were 290 by 40 by 19.4 feet.

Hungarian: The 2,190-ton steamship *Hungarian* left Liverpool for Portland, Maine, on February 8, 1860. She carried 205 people and the mail. On the morning of the 20th at about four o'clock her lights were seen from the shore at Cape Sable Island. The *Hungarian* was built in 1859 by W. Denny and Bros., owned and operated by the Allan Line and her dimensions were 298 by 38.5 by 17 feet.

HMS Blonde: The 32-gun war ship was wrecked on Blonde Rock on May 10, 1782, while on a voyage from Penobscot, Maine, to Halifax, Nova Scotia. The HMS *Blonde* was 704 tons, 132 feet long and 34.5 feet wide.

Libourne: The French cargo ship *Libourne* was sailing from Hampton Roads, Virginia, to Three Rivers with a cargo of coal on July 26, 1924, when she went ashore and was wrecked on Gull Ledge. The 4,186-ton *Libourne* was built in 1921 by W. Pickersgill and Sons. She was 364 by 52.9 by 24.3 feet and was equipped with triple expansion engines.

Mirjam: The 3,496-ton Norwegian ship *Mirjam* was wrecked September 23, 1923, on Seal Island while on a voyage from Portland, Maine, to Notre Dame Bay. She was built in 1904 by Caledon S.B. & E. Company. Her dimensions were 330 by 48 by 23.5 feet and she was equipped with triple expansion engines.

Moravian: The 3,567-ton British iron cargo ship *Moravian* wrecked on December 30, 1881, at Flat Island while on a voyage from Portland, Maine, to Liverpool, England. She was built in 1864 and operated by the Allan Line Steamship Co. Her dimensions were 389.3 by 39.5 by 32.1 feet. and she was equipped with compound inverted engines.

Navarra: Ship Registration No. 128283. The 4,387-ton British cargo ship *Navarra* was wrecked on Tusket Island on December 30, 1914, while on a voyage from Saint John, N.B., to Le Havre, France, carrying a cargo of hay and oats. She was built by R. Stephenson and Co. in 1909, equipped with triple expansion steam engines and her dimensions were 355.5 by 50 by 27.6 feet.

Ottawa: The 1,719-ton British cargo ship *Ottawa* wrecked on Blonde Rock near Seal Island on November 1, 1891. She was on a voyage from London, via Halifax to Saint John, N.B., carrying a general cargo. She was built by A. Stephen & Sons in 1891, equipped with triple expansion engines and her dimensions were 275.5 by 35.1 by 13 feet.

Orinoco: Ship Registration No. 112804. The 2,486-ton Canadian cargo ship *Orinoco* wrecked near Seal Island on July 26, 1907, while on a voyage to Halifax carrying a general cargo which also included sugar. She was built in 1888, owned and operated by Pickford & Black and her dimensions were 319.9 by 36.7 by 23.2 feet.

Para: The 1,103-ton British cargo ship *Para* struck a rock and foundered near Cape Sable on February 16, 1880, while on a voyage from Boston to Hartlepool carrying a general cargo. She was built in 1875, equipped with compound inverted engines and her measurements were 225.7 by 30.3 by 17 feet.

Peter Stuart: This 1,490-ton iron sailing ship under the command of Captain H. Hughes was wrecked near Yarmouth on July 3, 1892. Thirteen persons drowned including the captain's wife and child. *Peter Stuart* was built by A. McMillan and Sons in 1868 and her dimensions were 234 by 38.9 by 23 feet.

Sulina: The 2,379-ton British cargo ship *Sulina* was wrecked off Cape Sable on November 23, 1886, while on a voyage from Antwerp to Boston carrying a cargo of steel bars. She was built in 1884 by A. Leslie and Co., equipped with compound inverted engines and her dimensions were 301.4 by 38 by 24.7 feet.

8

Pirates and Privateers in Nova Scotia

Over the course of my research I came across so many references to pirates and privateers that I decided to include a
small chapter about them. They deliberately caused a great many
shipwrecks to occur off this coast. Nova Scotia was home to the
infamous "masterless men," the "shore pirates" and the "wreckers." These ruthless people deliberately lured many unsuspecting
ships ashore then murdered any surviving passengers and crew.
They would then strip the ship of its cargo, valuables and whatever else that was of use and could be salvaged from the wreck.
The business of "wrecking" was practiced extensively along the
coast of Nova Scotia for more than two hundred years and Cape
Breton Island has a history of piracy that can be traced back to
the 1400s.

The word *pirate* derives from Greek, meaning to attempt or
attack, and the Laws of Solon (c. 594 B.C.) refer to authorized
associations of pirates. They were sea-going outlaws, renegades
and/or mercenaries who sometimes hired their services and skills

out to the highest bidder. They played a lone hand against all comers without political purpose or official authority. A pirate captain, like a privateer captain, was an elected leader, liable to instant demotion if he had bad luck, not enough loot, or in the opinion of the company showed cowardice or bad judgment.

Privateers, on the other hand, were privately owned armed fighting ships. They were, in fact, pirates with a royal blessing and they were licensed to wage war on ships of a named foreign country. Such Licenses or Commissions were called Letters of Marque or Letters of Reprisal. Without one, a ship which used its armament offensively was guilty of piracy. In England the first Letters of Marque were issued in the thirteenth century, but for four hundred years after that the boundaries between legitimate trade, reprisal (privateering) and outright piracy were blurred, often to the point of invisibility. Here in Nova Scotia the recorded history of piracy and privateering dates back to the 1600s. Throughout the 1600s, the 1700s and well into the early 1800s piracy and privateering flourished.

It has been well documented that the captains and crews of these vessels (both pirate and privateer) often worked miracles of impudent and daring improvisation. And as for the men who crewed these infamous vessels, there existed very much an element of revenge or social rebellion as well as a greed for gold, even though there was no regular pay and for that matter no regular share in the profits. But a chance at riches and honour (and immediate treats of rum) often enticed fishermen, merchant seamen, adventurers and navy deserters to become pirates or privateers. Upwards of eighty men might be needed on a voyage, for fighting and to sail captured ships home.

Despite their achievements in charting coasts, currents and prevailing winds and their exploration of unknown regions, the pirates and the privateers never truly received the recognition that they may very well have deserved. Their remarkable feats of navigation and endurance in search of loot remain an inspiration, considering that the capture of a significant amount of treasure was fairly rare. Although a few obscure pirates may have been hanged from time to time, it is interesting to note that not a single pirate captain of notoriety or connections suffered more than a petty fine.

In 1801, special laws were enacted in Halifax to protect shipwrecked mariners and the official Receiver of Wrecks was given powers to shoot to kill anyone refusing aid to shipwrecked seamen. They were indeed tough laws for tough times. Pirates raided Sable Island and Seal Island even when Rescue Stations were established there. By 1830, so many buoys had been cut loose by pirates around Nova Scotia that extreme penalties were ordered for anyone approaching a navigational buoy.

In the mid 1970s evidence of a French pirate shipyard was discovered on the Mira River and about fifteen miles from Myra Gut there is a carved stone memorial to Captain William Kidd. The pirates used this shipyard as a safe haven and as a base to haul their ships and clean the hulls. They operated out of the Myra River for over a hundred years. According to the people of Trepassy, a Captain Roberts from Myra River sailed into Trepassy Bay, Newfoundland, and looted twenty-two ships in one day. The pirates left few records of their activities, but those who did refer to the safe harbour as St. Mary's and old maps show the Myra as St. Mary's River.

From November 16, 1756, to June 20, 1760, official records indicate that Letters of Marque were issued to sixteen vessels. The renewal of war with France in 1793 resulted in yet another period of privateering activity. By 1798 Great Britain faced a serious problem from losses in merchant shipping. In 1807 Britain was effectively cut off from timber supplies from the Baltic and was forced to turn to North American colonies for ships and timber. This led to the first great ship building period in the Maritimes.

The United States declaration of war on Great Britain in June 1812 resulted in the last and most active period of privateering. Between July 17, 1812, and January 24, 1815, the records indicate that thirty-one vessels were issued with Letters of Marque. From 1812 to 1815 more than 440 vessels, captured by privateers and Royal Navy ships and designated as prizes, were added to the registry book in the Maritime Provinces. A number were captured and recaptured several times. Nova Scotia was home to many of the most infamous and successful privateers in North America. Vessels like the HMS *Blonde* which wrecked on Blonde Rock, near Seal Island in 1782, the HMS *Rover,* which met her fate on the shores of Scatarie Island, Cape Breton, in 1778, and the more infamous *Liverpool Packet* have left their mark on our maritime history.

Halifax was also home to Enos Collins, a well-known merchant from Liverpool, Nova Scotia. He stands out as one of the most famous Nova Scotia privateers. He owned and operated the most dreaded Nova Scotia privateer ship during the war of 1812. His ship started out as a contraband slaver called the *Black Joke.* Seized by a British man-of-war, the sleek schooner was purchased by Collins; he fumigated her and christened her the *Liverpool Packet.* Under the command of Joseph Barss from Liverpool she sailed from Newfoundland to Cape Cod, taking more than thirty American ships in nine months. The *Liverpool Packet* was eventually captured by the Americans, then retaken by the British and purchased again by Collins.

His catches during the war totaled nearly a hundred ships, with prize money of more than a quarter of a million dollars. Collins, who had an interest in three separate privateers, made so much money, he founded Nova Scotia's first bank – the Halifax Banking Company. When he died in 1871, at the ripe old age of ninety-seven, he was one of the richest men in North America; his estate totaled six million dollars. Many of the cargoes captured by Nova Scotia privateers were stored before going to auction in the Privateers Warehouse, which is now part of Historic Properties on the Halifax waterfront.

Another lesser known sometimes pirate, sometimes privateer was a Frenchman named Pierre Morpain who also had a very colourful history and an equally fascinating story.

Born in Blaye, France, in1686, Pierre Morpain took to the sea at seventeen in 1703 after his parents died. He ended up in Saint-Domingue on the island of Hispaniola (now Haiti and the Dominican Republic) stalking British ships in Caribbean waters. By the time he was twenty, he was in command of his first vessel, Intrépide, and had extended his hunting grounds north to the New England coast.

With two British prize ships, Morpain made for the nearest French harbour - Port Royal, Nova Scotia. The beleaguered Acadians saw his unexpected arrival in August 1707 as divine intervention. Colonel John March and his New Englanders had besieged Port Royal earlier in the spring and the colony was running short of food. Shortly after Morpain's arrival, March and his army reappeared but were forced to retreat.

Morpain returned to the Caribbean but was back in Port Royal in August 1709 when he married Marie-Joseph Damours. He would return to Saint-Domingue only to fall out of favour with his employer, the governor of the colony, Marquis de Choiseul. It seems the governor did not appreciate prize ships and cargoes that should have gone to him ending up in the hands of Acadians in Port Royal. The British took Port Royal in 1710, but in 1711 Morpain turned up in another French outpost - Placentia, Newfoundland, where he continued his lucrative privateering ventures. While supplying the Acadian and Mi'kmaq resistance around Port Royal, Morpain was captured by the British and hauled to St. John's as a prisoner. He returned to France for a brief period in 1712.

Four years later, Morpain was back in Nova Scotia - this time in Louisbourg as port captain of Île Royale (Cape Breton Island), a position he held until 1745. In addition to administering the nautical interests of the French government in the area, such as ship construction and maintenance, salvage operations and navigation, he also acted as harbour pilot for the larger ships that called at various Cape Breton ports. By 1721 he had his first of several naval commissions in command of a storeship. His later commands included the Caribou and the Castor. He continued his privateering escapades against British and New England ships during these years.

Morpain played a crucial role in the first siege of Louisbourg in 1745, leading the demoralized garrison. Tired of the French presence and their threat to shipping, William Pepperell and his New Englanders camped on Louisbourg's doorstep. Morpain clashed with the regular French military commanders over strategy and was relieved of command. However, he distinguished himself to both sides with his energy and decisiveness. After the surrender, he was onboard one of the eleven ships which took the vanquished Louisbourg residents to France.

The cycle of war and peace between France and England continued, and the British handed Louisbourg and Cape Breton back to the French in 1748, much to the dismay of Pepperell and his colleagues. Morpain was offered his old job as port captain. Much to the relief of the New Englanders, the scourge of New England shipping didn't make it back to Louisbourg. Morpain died in Rochefort, France, in August 1749.

Both Enos Collins and Pierre Morpain played equally important parts in the history of Nova Scotia. Privateering and piracy were commonplace and a way of life for a great many people here for hundreds of years. Even today, in certain aspects of our everyday life it is still practiced and it still flourishes, albeit on a much smaller scale.

9

In Search of
Shipwrecks and Treasure

As a wreck diver I am often asked, How does one go about finding a shipwreck? What are the laws regarding treasure hunting and shipwreck salvage here in Nova Scotia? Can I keep what I find? There is no simple answer or explanation for any of these questions. So I will endeavour to explain some of my personal experiences, conversations with experts and personal observations of how things work here in Nova Scotia. I want to caution you that each scenario and situation that you may personally encounter will surely be as different and unique as every shipwreck you may seek to find. Questions from "who owns shipwrecks" to "artifact recovery" are still very hotly debated here in Nova Scotia. So much that formal papers have even been written and published by numerous people on this subject.

It's been called risky business, big business and serious business. No matter how you describe it, these words are never very far apart and they often describe the very essence of shipwreck salvage and treasure hunting. The business of searching for and salvaging shipwrecks has been both successful and lucrative for more than four hundred years, and to the person on the street it is probably considered more of an adventure for amateurs than a job for professional researchers and salvage teams. However, the vast majority of newcomers to this business lack several of the important factors necessary to succeed with the discovery and salvage of valuable shipwrecks.

Finding a shipwreck is a process that involves a combination of research, scientific search techniques, technology, time, and money. Searching for a shipwreck can be a very time-consuming, frustrating task with no guarantee of success even for the most ambitious and persistent hunters. In the seemingly infinite expanse of the ocean, even a shipwreck that is several hundred feet in length represents an incredibly minute target. Today, it is an indisputable fact that almost every significant discovery is made by a small number of dedicated teams consisting of skilled archivists and professional survey and diving teams, doing concentrated archival, survey and salvage work.

There are several important factors that have proven essential in almost every successful survey operation carried out. The first and the most important of these is archival research. Lack of sufficient archival research work is the single most common reason behind failure in the shipwreck hunting business. The most sophisticated survey equipment becomes useless without the prior knowledge of the essential historical documents of the shipwreck, such as a description of the ship, its position at the time of sinking, the circumstances behind its sinking, its cargo, and other critical details. These days there are only a handful of archival researchers in the world who have the knowledge and the experience to locate information about ships and their cargoes, and then correctly decipher the information that is often several hundred years old. Almost every significant recovery of treasure has first been discovered in the archives by a handful of competent marine historians and archival researchers.

Even after extensive research most shipwrecks and the remains of other marine disasters may not be exactly where investigations indicated they should be. Shipwrecks are where you find them. There are several reasons for this. First, inaccurate navigation owing to weather and the nature of the emergency makes it difficult, and sometimes nearly impossible, to know the exact location of the disaster. Second, from the time a position is obtained for the location, currents, wind and other factors may cause the wreck to drift. This drift may be several hundred feet to several miles from the recorded and reported site.

Equally important is the understanding of the technical aspects of a survey and salvage operation. Several teams have failed in their search while using sophisticated survey equipment due to the inability to interpret the gathered data correctly. It takes years to understand and to be able to interpret side scan sonar images. Many wrecks have been missed because side scan sonar operators were unable to differentiate between rock formations and a shipwreck. For example, when the cargo ship *Diana,* lost in the Malacca Strait, Indonesia, in 1817 with a cargo of porcelain, was finally discovered after several years of searching, it proved that the wreck had been passed over three times with a side scan sonar in the first season, but without anyone being able to interpret the images correctly.

The correct interpretation of side scan sonar data might be difficult, but even more so is the interpretation of magnetic anomalies. Today, there are only a few knowledgeable geophysicists who have a complete understanding of how the magnetic amplitude and curve is affected by the different size and shape of magnetic anomalies. In the past there was not a single survey/salvage company in the world that had the extensive knowledge of a skillful geophysicist, and still there are very few companies that include these knowledgeable people on their survey teams.

Another important factor in any successful project is the ability to deal with the legal aspects of the project correctly. In Nova Scotia the laws regulating commercial archaeology and salvage from shipwrecks are very complex, and there are many aspects that have to be considered before starting a project. Even some of the teams that employ a professional approach have encountered legal difficulties because they underestimated the legal problems before the salvage began. It is a common misconception that anything lost at sea is there for the taking. I can tell you from personal experience that this is not the case. Anyone even contemplating the excavation or salvage of a shipwreck must understand the legal situation very thoroughly. In addition, the cultural, environmental and historical impact of a discovery must be considered with respect to all of the interested parties. Any shipwreck project should only be undertaken with the full cooperation and approval of the provincial government where the site is located. Only after a mutually acceptable agreement has been reached should a project be undertaken.

Nevertheless, with the exception of Louisbourg Harbour, it is not illegal to dive on known shipwrecks here in Nova Scotia and no permit or paperwork is required to do so. However, according to the Nova Scotia Museum of Natural History, anyone specifically searching for a shipwreck requires a permit. Nova Scotia is also unique, in that no other province in Canada has a Treasure Trove Act or a Special Places Protection Act.

Three pieces of legislation are very important and apply specifically to shipwrecks here in Nova Scotia: the Canada Shipping Act, the Nova Scotia Special Places Protection Act, and the Nova Scotia Treasure Trove Act. You will require special licenses and permits, and any professional endeavours will also require the services of a marine lawyer and a marine archaeologist.

The Canada Shipping Act is federal legislation that pertains to all wrecks, including historical wrecks. By this statute, anything recovered from a wreck must be turned over to the Receiver of Wrecks until ownership can be determined. Failure to do so can bring heavy fines. This act is administered by the Canadian Coast Guard for the Ministry of Fisheries and Oceans. In addition, the Navigable Waters Act ensures that there is no disruption to shipping as a result of activities licensed under the Nova Scotia Treasure Trove Act.

The Nova Scotia legislature passed the Special Places Protection Act in 1980 and amended it in 1989 to provide for the preservation, regulation and study of archaeological and historical remains and palaeontological and ecological sites. This act requires you to have a Heritage Research Permit from the Special Places Program, Department of Tourism, Culture and Heritage before disturbing any place where historical artifacts may be found, including underwater sites.

The Treasure Trove Act was proclaimed in 1954 initially to govern activities on Oak Island. Treasure trove is defined as "precious stones or metals in a state other than their natural state." It has been the responsibility of the Nova Scotia Department of Natural Resources, formerly the Department of Mines and Energy, since 1979.

If you intend to search for, excavate and/or salvage a shipwreck, there are several options open to you. One option is to locate the true owner of the ship and/or its cargo and negotiate a deal to purchase or salvage the vessel and/or its cargo from them. It may very well be an insurance company, a private company or a foreign government. Most vessels that were wrecked from the early 1900s onwards can be traced to their true owners. However, for most ships wrecked prior to the 1900s, the true owners cannot be traced.

If you have reason to believe the vessel carried a valuable cargo and if you intend to search for and salvage that cargo and if a true owner cannot be found, another option would be to apply for a treasure trove license for the area the shipwreck is located in. In Nova Scotia, this is how the process works.

The first thing to do is to make an application to the Department of Natural Resources for a Treasure Trove License for the specific area you are interested in. The application will also require a detailed work plan. Once all the necessary documents have been submitted, the application will go forward through the proper channels and eventually to the Executive Council (Cabinet) for their consideration and approval. The cost to make an application is $500. The entire process can take as long as six months to a year, even longer in some cases, and there is no guarantee that it will be approved.

If it is not a modern shipwreck and the true owners cannot be located, the next step is to make an application to the Special Places Program of the Department of Tourism, Culture and Heritage for a Heritage Research Reconnaissance Permit. There is no cost to make an application. It provides the right to explore for wrecks within a given area, and it is the bare minimum needed to obtain a Treasure Trove License. This is a permit class given to non-archaeologists or to archaeologists doing general work, and does not allow for disturbance of the site.

If a shipwreck is found and the treasure trove license holder wants to excavate it, he or she will have to employ a marine archaeologist, as the Nova Scotia Museum will require an objective assessment as to the condition and significance of the wreck. This must be done by a qualified (and Nova-Scotia-Museum-approved) marine archaeologist under a Heritage Research Archaeological Resource Impact Assessment Permit. The marine archaeologist then delivers a report that describes the resource in such terms needed to assess the archaeological and historical significance of the wreck. Depending on the results, a full range of options is available, from complete avoidance to salvage. If any type of archaeological excavation is required, an Archaeological Research Permit is required with qualified (and Nova-Scotia-Museum-approved) personnel, conservation plans, etc. Also, it is important to note that a company or corporation cannot hold a permit; it must be an individual leading the project and the person who writes the report.

When a treasure trove is discovered on the seabed and actually recovered through the legal and scientific process described above, it must be turned over to the Receiver of Wrecks for a period of one year and a day. Then it is further held on to by the Department of Natural Resources for up to another six months until a royalty is chosen by representatives of the Nova Scotia Museum.

With respect to royalty selection, the province gets a 10 percent royalty of the treasure trove, chosen as a representative sample. All non-treasure trove artifacts recovered (including any bronze artifacts) automatically belong to the province and must be documented, conserved (at your expense), and delivered to the Nova Scotia Museum where they become part of the provincial collection. Also, a box fee is charged to cover some of the costs for long term storage of artifacts.

Remember for thousands of years, the world's wealth travelled by water. Some of the wealth that has gone down with nineteenth- and twentieth-century freighters dwarfs what was lost on the pay ships, galleons and other ships of the eighteenth and nineteenth century. There are many World War II cargo ships and freighters that sank off the coast of Nova Scotia. As part of their war cargo most of them carried very precious metals like zinc, brass, nickel, iron, steel, lead, platinum, aluminum, magnesium, copper, and some even carried gold. In most cases, the cargo of a Second World War ship can be purchased from its current owner (an insurance company or the government) and legally salvaged. In Nova Scotia some of the world's lost treasures lie in fairly shallow waters, often within sight of land, lightly covered in sand and silt. The owners have long departed this world, many perishing in the very storms that sent their precious belongings to the bottom of the sea. Time and tide have obliterated their memory from history.

Many treasure wrecks rest beneath the waves for centuries waiting to be salvaged, their cargoes worth thousands of times more today than when they were lost.

Deep Water Shipwrecks

Some treasure lies far off shore, in the deep, dark waters beyond the continental shelf. Those wrecks usually lie on the bottom with hardly a trace of overlying silt or sediment. The ice-cold, still ocean depths protect them from decomposition and dispersal. These ships, blown off course by raging storms and swirling seas, drifted far from the trading routes before disappearing into the depths without leaving a soul to tell the tale. Advancements in modern undersea technology stand out as the most important development behind the recent boom in shipwreck salvage and treasure hunting. The availability of high-resolution digital side scan sonar systems and low-cost magnetometers have revolutionized the age-old quest for treasure. It is now possible to detect and recover sunken treasures from depths unimaginable even a few years ago. Remote Operated Vehicles can dive several miles beneath the ocean waves. Side scan sonar can probe the deepest marine trenches and identify the remains of long-lost vessels waiting to be salvaged.

Deep water shipwrecks have also attracted the interest and financial backing of Wall Street for a number of reasons. Archaeologists need commercial financing to reach deep sites and depth

DeepWorker is a submersible capable of diving to 2,000 feet.
It has a number of marine applications, including searching for deep
water wrecks. Its inventor, Nuytco Research Ltd. based in British
Columbia, is a world leader in the development and operation of
undersea technology. (Photo courtesy of Nuytco Research Ltd.)

is a barrier to all but well-funded commercial operations. High
costs dictate professionalism in commercial operations. As well,
high-tech operations increase public and media interest. Deep
shipwrecks tend to be in one capsule, not scattered, and the difficulty of access provides good site security; in addition, such sites
have probably not been previously salvaged. Due to low oxygen
and light levels in the deep ocean, artifacts are often in an amaz-
ing state of preservation, and not encrusted with coral.

In 1986 the Columbus America Discovery Group out of Ohio,
U.S.A., used the most current technology available at the time to
locate and salvage a gold shipment from the SS *Central America*,
which sank in eight thousand feet of water more than two hundred miles off the coast of South Carolina. A law suit between

C.A.D.G. and numerous insurance companies dragged through the American court system for several years.

Florida-based Odyssey Marine, a leader in the field of deep ocean shipwreck exploration, located and successfully excavated the side-wheel steamer SS *Republic*, which sank in 1865 while en route from New York to New Orleans after battling a hurricane for two days. Odyssey Marine spent twelve years searching for the *Republic*, using side scan sonar, magnetometers and robots to search 1,500 square miles of ocean. They finally discovered the shipwreck 1,700 feet below the surface of the Atlantic Ocean, approximately a hundred miles off the Georgia coast.

The commercial archaeological excavation of the shipwreck began in November of 2003 and is still continuing. Among the 17,000 coins already retrieved are numerous gold eagles, gold double eagles, silver half dollars and even a few quarters, nearly all dating between the 1840s and 1865. Unlike other recently salvaged shipwrecks, a wide variety of dates and mints have been noted in this find. The find is estimated to be worth $180 million. Odyssey Marine purchased the rights to salvage the wreck from the original insurance company, which paid out the original claim in 1865.

Most recently Odyssey Marine searched over four hundred square miles of ocean before it located the HMS *Sussex* in three thousand feet of water. HMS *Sussex* was a large 80-gun English warship lost in a severe storm in 1694. The story of her mission and place in the unfolding events of the late seventeenth and early eighteenth centuries presents a fascinating scenario to archaeologists, historians, and those with a general interest in European and international developments. Built in the reign of William and Mary, HMS *Sussex* was escorting a large merchant fleet to the Mediterranean when she was lost. Research indicates that her admiral also had orders to pay a large sum of money to the Duke of Savoy to continue the war against France. Evidence suggests that the payment, consisting of nine tons of gold coins, was lost with the ship. If the research is correct, then the numismatic value estimates for the cargo could be worth up to four billion dollars or more.

Another inherent characteristic of all underwater survey and salvage operations is the large financial risk involved. This risk, however, is balanced by the possibilities of phenomenal profits if a project becomes successful. The risk for the weekend treasure hunter is practically nothing – a bit of scuba equipment, a boat and some time spent reading books and looking over some maps. But wreck hunting and recovery are what you make of it. Those who choose to seek bigger rewards must take bigger risks. A mentor of mine, my former high school teacher Hardy Kalberlah, once told me, "It takes two things to find shipwrecks, time and money. Usually, when you have one, you don't have the other."

These days there are many companies offering investment opportunities to persons interested in taking part in the fascinating business of shipwreck recovery. For those that do offer investment opportunities, the expected return on invested capital, time or resources into a reputable company can be as much as five to twenty times that of the investment, if the company succeeds in one or several of its projects. It can also be a huge financial loss, and as a wise man once told me, "Invest only what you can afford to lose."

The shipwreck exploration and salvage business is generally viewed by most financial planners and investors as "extremely speculative" and of "exceptionally high risk." Although an exploration company may have access to a substantial amount of research and data compiled regarding various projects and the shipwreck business, the quality and reliability of such research and data, like all research and data of its nature, is unknown. Even if the company is able to plan and obtain permits for its projects, there is a possibility that the shipwreck(s) may have been previously salvaged, or may not have had anything of value onboard at the time of the sinking. Even if objects of believed value are located and recovered, there is the possibility that the company's rights to the recovered objects will be challenged by others, including private parties and government entities asserting conflicting claims.

Finally, even if the company is successful in locating and retrieving objects from a shipwreck and establishing good title thereto, there can be no assurance as to the value that such objects will bring at their sale, as the market for such objects is very uncertain.

Investing in the shipwreck exploration, recovery and development business is without question risky business. But for those who do roll the dice, the potential return on investment can be staggering. Investing in the hunt for a lost shipwreck and sunken treasure also provides the vicarious thrill of being part of the search, part of the dream, and part of the ultimate adventure. Today, there are many business people and savvy investors who look at this field as one with real investment potential and a serious return on investment.

10

Discoveries in Waiting

There are still a great many discoveries to be made here in Nova Scotia. Hundreds of lost shipwrecks are documented and many are known to have carried treasure and other valuable cargo wrecked off this coast. Many are not documented, simply because there were no survivors. I have chosen to touch on only a few of these lost shipwrecks.

As previously mentioned the first recorded shipwreck to occur on Cape Breton Island was the 70-ton *Chancewell*, wrecked on June 23, 1597. Historians, scholars and shipwreck enthusiasts have narrowed the suspected site of this wreck down to two possible areas: St. Ann's Bay or Ingonish. It has never been found and while not a treasure ship, its historical significance is of paramount importance. The following are some of the other documented but undiscovered shipwrecks.

Le Governor Du War, a French First Rate ship with seventy guns, wrecked somewhere between Green Island and Sampson Cove in the early 1700s.

On September 8, 1711, four British transports, HMS *Feversham*, HMS *Neptune*, HMS *Mary* and HMS *Joseph,* left New York as part of Admiral Sir Hovden Walker's fleet bound for Quebec. All four ships were wrecked on October 7 in a bay to the west of Scatarie Island. Alex Storm and Adrian Richards discovered HMS *Feversham* on September 7, 1968. To date the other three transports have not yet been found. Part of their cargo was gold coins and very rare silver American Colonial coins from the 1600s known as Pine Tree Shillings.

The *La Liberte* was a French frigate, lost on December 11, 1719, off St. Esprit, Cape Breton, carrying $500,000 in gold and silver bullion. There is a reference to this shipwreck in *Fell's Guide to Sunken Treasure Ships of the World* by Lieutenant Harry E. Rieseberg and A.A. Mikalow, published in 1965. There is a second reference in the *Canadian Weekend Magazine* No. 18, 1966.

Le Triton

Probably the richest ship to wreck in this hemisphere is *Le Triton* and it has yet to be found. In the vast expanse of the ocean somewhere off the southeast coast of Cape Breton Island lie the remains of one of the richest shipwrecks in the world, worth millions of dollars.

After the second siege, when the English took possession of Fortress Louisbourg, they shrewdly kept the French flag flying to lure in unsuspecting French shipping. On June 22, 1745, the English captured the *Charmante*, a 28-gun French East India ship. A few days later they captured another, the *Heron*. From her crew they learned of two more treasure ships a few days behind, the *Le Triton* and the *Notre Dame De La Delivrance*. Both were en route from Bengal, India, via Lima, Peru, to Louisbourg and finally to France. A few days later the English captured the 22-gun *Notre Dame De La Delivrance*. The English war ship *Canterbury* took the captured treasure onboard for shipment home and the riches were recorded in the captain's log as follows:

      39 bags containing 1,000 coins

      9 bags, each containing 300 doubloons in gold (2,700 gold coins)

      3 boxes containing 2,000 coins per box (6,000 coins)

      1 box containing 1,000 coins

      7 pigs of virgin silver

32 boxes containing 2000 pieces of silver
1 box containing 1140 doubloons
18 bars of gold – each bar weighs 65 lbs
1,000 coins in silver
22 chests each containing 2,000 coins
51 chests each containing 3,000 coins

Le Triton was never captured; it wrecked in a hurricane on the southeast coast of Cape Breton. There were some survivors who made it ashore and with the help of the local Indians eventually made their way to Quebec. This is how the wreck became known.

As Alex Storm pointed out in his book *Seaweed and Gold,* the documentation is very skimpy and sparse, but there are some reports and eye witness accounts of a "Spanish Galleon" type of ship, wrecking off the coast around the same time. The warship *Le St. Michel*, had been dispatched from France to search for, intercept and protect the four French East India Company ships, including the 600-ton, 28-gun *Le Triton* which had onboard as much or more than the *Notre Dame De La Delivrance*. The *Le St. Michel* was also carrying 48,000 pieces of silver and 2,000 gold coins to pay the troops at Louisbourg. It was wrecked in the same hurricane.

Le Triton was owned or chartered by the French La Compagnie des Indes Occidentales. She was listed as a Vaisseau; lightly armed, these types of ships usually carried some twenty to twenty-two cannons, mostly for self-defense purposes. She was built between 1727-28 and taken off the list in 1745, presumably after her loss. La Compagnie des Indes Occidentales was liquidated in 1769.

HMS Tilbury

The HMS *Tilbury* was a Third Rate Frigate or Man-of-War and, in its day, was one of the finest ships in the entire fleet. Designed by Pierson Lock and built at Portsmouth in 1745, the 1,124-ton, 147-foot vessel carried sixty guns.

HMS *Tilbury* was one of four pay ships carrying thirty-four chests of coins for Rear Admiral Edward Boscawen and Vice Admiral Francis Holburne's fleet of twenty ships, which consisted of fourteen Men-of-War and six frigates. On Sunday, September 25, 1757, the entire fleet was en route to Louisbourg when, as it approached the south coast of Cape Breton, a gale sprang up. Later through the night they found themselves in a full-blown hurricane that was raging off the island's southeast coast.

The HMS *Tilbury* was lost in the hurricane in the middle of the night. Wreckage and survivors from the *Tilbury* were found a few miles north of St. Esprit, on the southeast coast of Cape Breton. At the time of her loss, she was commanded by Captain Henry Barnsley who perished together with 120 of his crew. When *Tilbury* wrecked she had onboard four hundred people; only 280 men survived and were able to swim ashore. It is believed that *Ferret* foundered near Halifax as no wreckage or survivors were ever found. HMS *Ferret* was launched May 10, 1743, and fitted as a ship sloop in 1755 with fourteen guns and fourteen swivel cannons. At the time of her disappearance she was commanded by Captain Francis Upton.

Research, including excerpts from the journal of *L'Inflexible* and the journal of *Le Formidable* in 1757, provided the following information and clues. "Tuesday September 27, 1757. A vessel arrived in Louisbourg from Port Toulouse and reported that yesterday they saw 2 vessels dismasted. That same afternoon a boat from Canceaux [Canso] arrived in Louisbourg and reported having found a vessel with two tiers of guns aground at St. Esprit and they recognized her as English. The prow of the vessel was all that could be seen. On it there were more than 100 men. They saw a good many who had escaped to the shore. The Governor dispatched 150 soldiers from Louisbourg to take them prisoner.

"Wednesday September 28, 1757. Wind S.W. all day pretty fresh. This morning a boat arrived from the vicinity of St. Esprit having onboard the 1st. Lieutenant [John Thane] of the Man of War, the *Tilbury*, 58 guns, lost on that coast on Sunday. He came to ask for help for about 200 men who had escaped from the wreck; the prisoner and the men who brought him here testify that they saw some other wrecked vessels and many dismasted; a Council was held this afternoon to decide whether we should go in search of the disabled vessels, which the winds we have had cannot have carried far from the land; the hope of saving *Le Tonnant* by giving it all the assistance the squadron can afford prevailed; and only the *La Fleur De Lys* was sent out for Canceaux [Canso].

"Saturday, October 1, 1757. The wind varied every day from W.N.W. to S.W. Two merchant ships left for St. Domingo along the south coast. The debris of vessels have been found, from which it is believed that two others are lost.

"Wednesday, October 5, 1757. Yesterday and today there are a number of prisoners from the Tilbury; 280 men in all were saved; debris are being found continually along the coast; according to the information we possess 3 large vessels and 1 Frigate are lost between St. Esprit and Louisbourg.

"Saturday, October 22, 1757. The wind W.S.W. to W., fine weather. This morning there arrived 6 Indians with 2 Englishmen captured at Halifax who informed us of the arrival in that port of 14 vessels of Holburne's squadron, two of them without any masts. They had information of the loss of the *Tilbury* and of another large vessel, but seemed to have no news of the rest of the squadron."

It is interesting to note that, as mentioned in the ship's log, one of the survivors from HMS *Tilbury* was Senior First Lieutenant John Thane. Further research indicates that he appeared to be quite talented and very knowledgeable about the coast of Cape Breton, as he was taken prisoner by the French and his scheduled exchange for a trade with the English for a French prisoner was deferred for quite some time.

While the *Tilbury* was in fact one of the four pay ships for Vice Admiral Holburne's fleet, I could not locate any specific, detailed information relating to the actual cargo onboard at the time. The only reference I was able to locate, after scouring the public archives and throughout my entire letter writing campaign and correspondence to Ottawa and England, were some letters and dispatches that read: "34 chests of silver coins was sent to

North America aboard the *Devonshire, Edinburgh, Superbe* and *Tilbury*." I was able to locate and acquire a detailed copy of the building plans and line drawings for HMS *Tilbury*. There is also a reference on pages 209 and 210 of J.S. McLennen's book *Louisbourg From its Foundation to its Fall 1713-1758*, first published in London in 1918.

Today on a marine navigational map of Cape Breton Island, just south of Forchu and a little north of St. Peters, you will find Cape St. Esprit. Very nearby you will note a place marked on the map called Tilbury Rocks. This is the spot where part of the HMS *Tilbury* actually came ashore. What was left of the bow and mid section of the wreck was first discovered by Alex Storm and Adrian Richards on July 19, 1969. For many years (right up until the 1980s) there was an old cannon lying about the shoreline mixed in with the rocks. Eventually the cannon was removed by a local doctor and transported by a team of oxen to St. Peters, but today there is no trace of it.

In 1986, after three years of searching, a Montreal-based dive team headed by Pierre Le Clerce and Gilles Brisebois recovered more than eight hundred silver coins, dated from 1730 to 1755, from a wreck in thirty feet of water off the coast of Cape Breton that they believed to be part of HMS *Tilbury*. They accounted for many, but not all, of the cannons and they did not locate the stern or forecastle section of the wreck. To date no one has. It is in that section where the eight chests of coins and many other valuables will be found.

The Holland Map of 1767

In 1766, Captain Samuel Holland was commissioned to carry out a survey and create an accurate map of Cape Breton Island. Somewhere near what is today called Pleasant Bay he noted several ships' masts sticking up out of the water. How these wrecks came to be is not known, as there were no survivors nor has any existing documentation or research been unearthed that would offer more information. Holland noted the exact location of these wrecks and included these observations as "Several

Wrecks Here" on his finished map. To date no one has discovered exactly where the wrecks are, what nationality they are or what they were carrying for cargo.

The Empire Manor

The *Empire Manor* wrecked off the coast during World War II when it was accidentally rammed by another ship. The *Empire Manor* broke in two and sank in three hundred feet of water more than a hundred miles off Newfoundland. On board, mixed in with her war cargo, were eighty gold ingots. Each ingot weighed approximately seventy-two pounds (do the math). After the war, the first salvage attempt was unsuccessful, but a second attempt many years later in 1973 succeeded and seventy-two of the gold ingots were recovered. The other eight gold bars are still out there somewhere in the bow section, waiting to be recovered.

11

Wreck Hunting
Tools and Techniques

There are many different schools of thought on how to best search for and find a shipwreck. I personally have two favourite methods that I subscribe to. Depending on the amount of resources and time involved, I can tell you from personal experience that both techniques will in fact work. The first is the shotgun approach, which refers to searching a very large area with the purpose of locating a specific shipwreck or shipwrecks. The second is called the rifle approach, which refers to narrowing down the search to a smaller specific area by using more information and resources. Each approach is different. Depending on your particular set of circumstances you may favour one over the other.

Regardless of which approach you choose, you will need some type of a plan, some shipwreck information, and access to some resources. A few other desirable personal traits that will enhance your chances of success are persistence and tenacity. Sources of shipwreck research can range from information supplied by local fishermen to more in-depth research from the

144

archives or local libraries. As with any type of research project, you will only get out of it what you put into it, hence the two final and most important ingredients that can make or break any shipwreck search: the amount of time and money allotted to carry out the project.

There are various techniques and equipment that can be used on a specific project, depending on how much time and money you have access to. There are several tools and techniques that I've used over the years to find shipwrecks.

Swimming searches tend to work well in areas where the visibility is very good or exceptional. There are various patterns that a diver can swim using a compass and a line. They work best when there are a group of divers involved but they are very time consuming.

Tow boards are an excellent tool than can be deployed from a small Zodiac or even a Cape Island fishing boat. The diver hangs on to the board and is towed along at a comfortable speed. Again, this type of tool works best when the area you are searching has very clear water.

A typical fishing dory or fiberglass skiff can be modified or fitted with Plexiglas panels and converted into a glass-bottom boat. This works very well in areas where the water is shallow and clear. Depending on the weather, you can stay out all day and cover a great deal of coastline searching for signs of a shipwreck.

An onboard-ship/boat echo or depth sounder is another useful tool. These electronic devices can be found aboard just about every type of fishing and recreational boat. They do, however, project a very narrow sonar beam, which means you would literally have to pass right over a wreck in order to see it. Also, the wreck would have to have some shape or structure sticking up from the seabed.

Boat-towed or drop cameras can be very useful if you have unlimited access to a boat. Again, you need to be using them in fairly clear water, but they can produce excellent results. They are inexpensive and very user friendly.

Underwater Metal Detectors

Underwater metal detectors are very affordable and useful tools when searching for something that may be buried under gravel, rock or sand. The vast majority of ships wrecked in the eighteenth and nineteenth centuries were made of wood, but all wooden shipwrecks had metal of some type aboard that was used in the construction process, such as brass or bronze spikes, anchors, rigging, copper nails and copper sheathing on the hull, and pig iron ballast, to name a few. Warships carried swords, tomahawks, boarding axes, cannons, cannon balls, and musket shot. Then there were the personal items of the people who made up the crew and passengers of these ships; most had cutlery, utensils, coinage and jewelry. In almost all cases these items would be lost during a shipwreck.

An underwater metal detector will detect ferrous metals such as iron and steel. Just as a magnetometer will detect the presence of large metal objects from a distance of several hundred yards, an underwater metal detector will detect metal objects (depending on the size) from several inches to several feet, even if the entire wreck is covered in sand or buried in gravel. Once the wreck site has been located, underwater metal detectors can be used to find specific parts of the ship and cargo that may still be buried. You can also use your underwater metal detector year round in any type of weather, on land, in the surf, on beaches as well as underwater.

Metal detectors work because metal conducts electricity. Metal detectors create an electromagnetic field which penetrates the ground or seabed. When the search coil senses a change in this field (caused by a metal object) it sends a signal back to the control box which then alerts the operator. Metal detectors react to the surface area of objects, not their mass; therefore, the larger the object, the deeper it can be detected.

Measured in kilohertz (kHz), the frequency is the number of times a signal is transmitted into the ground or seabed and received back, per second. The lower the frequency used by the detector, the deeper it can normally penetrate. At low frequencies, however, the sensitivity to small targets is sometimes reduced. The

A Minelab Excalibur 1000 underwater metal detector.
(Image courtesy of Minelab USA)

higher the frequency, the higher the sensitivity to small objects, but it may not penetrate as deeply.

Soil contains naturally occurring salts and minerals, which is known as mineralization. Areas of highly mineralized soil are generally known as difficult soils. Sand or loam soils are low in minerals and are usually very easy to detect. Most metal detectors have a "ground balance" which is used to compensate for the effect of mineralization. Automatic ground tracking (AGT) refers to the ability of the detector to track the changes in the ground mineralization and automatically adjust the ground balance to suit. This ensures perfect ground balance and full detection depth and eliminates the need for the operator to stop and manually adjust the detector as the ground conditions change.

The coil sends an electromagnetic field into the ground and receives a response that is interpreted by the control box. The size of the coil can affect the depth at which a target can be detected, or the sensitivity to that target. Coils can also have different search patterns, depending on how they are made. The two most common types of coil are the "double D" and the "mono-loop" which give the greatest detection coverage, depth and highest level of overall performance. By changing the size or design of the coil, the detector can become more versatile for changing conditions.

Discrimination refers to the ability of the metal detector to estimate the type of metal a target is made of. Discrimination gives you the ability to ignore unwanted objects like pull tabs or beer caps, while detecting for valuable items made from metals like gold, silver, brass or copper.

Most detectors operate on one or sometimes two frequencies only. Broad band spectrum technology automatically transmits seventeen separate frequencies over a range of 1.5 kHz to 25.5 kHz. This means you have more depth, greater sensitivity and more accurate discrimination.

I have used a Minelab Excalibur underwater metal detector for years. The Excalibur is without a doubt the finest engineered and packaged, totally waterproof, discrimination metal detector on the market today. It also has five different control settings, which require a bit of learning and experimenting. However, this unique design allows it to be tuned and adjusted on the surface, beach-combing or underwater searching a wreck site. The Excalibur is a very compact unit in dive mode, and underwater it becomes an extension of your arm. A target when located is just under and in front of you, no need to reach or swim forward. The unit is non-buoyant and will, if released, lie flat on the bottom of the seabed – no fighting to keep it down or close to the bottom.

Diver Propulsion Vehicle (DPV)

The Diver Propulsion Vehicle (DPV) is a vehicle with an integral saddle that the diver physically rides. DPVs have been available in various configurations for nearly three decades, but until recently, they were used primarily by the military and com-mercial divers. Today, more and more recreational divers are becoming interested in DPVs. A DPV allows for extended diving range. Trying to swim or fin three to five miles on a dive is not practical nor is it possible for the average diver. However, with a DPV the average diver can cover this distance on a single dive and because the diver will use less energy, it is possible to con-serve breathing gas and extend the time of the dive. The DPV allows the diver to cover more territory and see more of the

Wreck divers using Farallon Mk7-E Diver Propulsion Vehicles
(Image courtesy of Farallon USA)

underwater world with increased comfort and maneuverability. Some divers use the DPV to find shipwrecks. Others use it to get to a specific shipwreck site, where they tie off the DPV, continue their dive and pick up the DPV for the ride back to their origination point.

Some wrecks are large with open spaces that can safely accommodate a diver riding a DPV. For the wreck diver, range and comfort are very important. Thus a DPV with a long range and a saddle for comfort is very desirable. Riding a DPV for the first time is like taking that first breath underwater: it is exciting and addictive. You can cover large areas of a diving environment during a single tank dive. It is an awesome experience. At the end of the dive you will feel relaxed and comfortable, having experienced much less of the fatigue normally associated with long exploratory dives. It is the best way to travel underwater, especially when searching for shipwrecks. Boat diving with a DPV is another unique and pleasant experience. You will cover more area than ever before, enhancing the value of your dive beyond your wildest dreams.

Today, the interest among recreational and technical divers continues to grow, and awareness and education on the subject of DPVs is increasing dramatically. Several national scuba training agencies now offer specialty courses and certification. If you are purchasing a DPV for the first time and you do not have any experience with these vehicles, it is important to seek professional training. Initial training should be conducted in a confined and controlled water environment, such as a swimming pool.

Learning to ride a DPV is just like any other scuba skill; it should be perfected before taking the DPV to open water. A DPV is an excellent tool and investment for anyone who is searching for shipwrecks. It is user friendly, cost effective, low maintenance and can be used year round.

Remote Operated Vehicle (ROV)

ROV is an acronym for Remote Operated Vehicle or Robotic Operated Vehicle. These vehicles are powered by electric thrusters and they can literally fly through the water column in any direction, horizontally or vertically. They are usually equipped with high-powered underwater lights systems, a high resolution video and/or still camera, a sonar navigation system and some even have manipulator robotic arms. They are tethered to the surface via an umbilical cord which supplies the power necessary to operate the machine.

Some types of ROVs can dive as deep as fifteen thousand feet. Most all types can stay down for an unlimited amount of time and as such they offer a cost effective and safer alternative to deep water diving and survey operations. They are not affected by water temperature or depth. Additionally, they can operate in all types of different environmental conditions, from the sunny Caribbean to the sub-zero arctic conditions at the North Pole, with no risk or danger to human life and an unlimited bottom time in a day or night environment. For these reasons they make an excellent tool for searching for and surveying deep water shipwrecks.

This Phantom DHD2+2 ROV is equipped with an on board Kongsberg sonar, digital still and video camera and a manipulator, it is capable of diving to 2000 feet and is owned and operated by Deep Sea Equipment Inc, a marine equipment rental company in Halifax, Nova Soctia.

Marine Magnetometer

The marine magnetometer is, without question, the most indispensable tool for shipwreck hunting due to its low cost and its ability to detect magnetic objects at distances much greater than conventional metal detectors. A magnetometer is a passive instrument that measures the strength of the earth's magnetic field.

Magnetic materials, such as iron objects common to shipwreck sites, will cause a local change in the earth's magnetic field. This amount of change (or size of anomaly) is related to several factors, including the mass of magnetic material, how magnetic the material is, and distance from the material. The modern magnetometer can detect these relatively small changes in the earth's magnetic field with high sensitivity. Recorded data can then be used to accurately locate the source of the disturbance (i.e., the shipwreck) and also determine its size. In general, the more iron material on a shipwreck the larger anomaly it will create and the further away it can be detected.

Unlike sonar instruments, a magnetometer is able to detect objects even if they are buried deep below the seabed. The modern marine magnetometer consists of an underwater housing (often resembling a torpedo) that contains a magnetic sensor and driving electronics. This unit is often referred to as a towfish or fish since it is towed a distance behind the ship underwater. The

John Shumacher prepares to deploy a magnetometer on the hunt for the stern section of the *Auguste*. (Photo by Terry Dwyer)

fish is towed by a high-strength insulated cable, which is also used to receive data and communicate with the magnetometer.

There are a variety of data-logging options. The simplest in use is a streaming hardcopy printout of the measured variation in the magnetic field strength plotted as a line graph. A marine magnetometer allows you to connect the magnetometer to a personal computer for real time plotting of the measured magnetic field and digital logging of the data to text files. Global Positioning System (GPS) receivers can also be added to modern systems to provide position data with every magnetic reading. Another major feature is that it can combine the magnetometer with an integral navigator plotter. Simply connecting a GPS navigator to the magnetometer allows a plotter to be used. When searching for a wreck, the boat's position is continuously displayed on the screen, while the track of the boat is recorded to show the

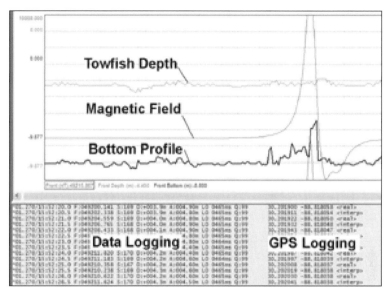

An example of the current software available from Marine Magnetics.
(Image courtesy of Marine Magnetics)

areas already covered. To help pinpoint a wreck's exact position, electronic buoys can be placed on the screen to mark significant positions in the survey area. This combination of magnetometer and plotter in one unit gives the optimum wreck location.

The biggest difference between the various magnetometers on the market is the way that the magnetic sensor operates. The type of magnetic sensor in a magnetometer often determines its performance characteristics. A magnetometer is classified by the type of magnetic sensor it contains. There are basically three different types of magnetometer on the market and often used by the shipwreck hunting community. They are the Proton magnetometer, the Cesium magnetometer and the Overhauser magnetometer.

Because of its sheer simplicity, reliability and accuracy, the Overhauser marine magnetometer is, in my opinion, clearly the best choice. It's used by more government agencies, the offshore geophysical industry and professional treasure hunting companies all over the world. Ontario-based Marine Magnetics Corp. is the only company in the world manufacturing marine magnetometers that use the Overhauser sensors.

Side Scan Sonar

These days well-funded shipwreck hunters are turning to side scan sonar to search the seabed for lost shipwrecks. Side scan uses high-energy sound beams, bounced off the bottom, to send back a picture-like image of the seafloor. The beam is a narrow one-degree in width and fans out about forty-five degrees horizontally per side. Depending on the frequency, the swath covered on each pass can be as wide as two thousand feet at low resolution (50 kHz) or nine hundred feet at high resolution (600 kHz). This is a very effective method to cover large areas of the ocean in a short time. The acoustic signal is transmitted by a transducer towfish, towed behind the search vessel. This eliminates any distortion caused by the pitch and roll of the vessel.

The first sonar systems were developed during World War I by American, British and French military forces to detect submarines. They were called ASDIC for Anti-Submarine Detection Investigation Committee. Side scan sonar was first developed by Dr. Harold Edgerton at the Massachusettes Institute of Technology in the 1960s. Since then, technology has improved and better methods of transmitting, receiving and processing the signal have been developed. Current machines utilize digital signal processing where the signal is digitized within the towfish and sent to the processor via a Kevlar-reinforced fiber optic cable, reducing signal loss and radio interference. This allows for convenient display and digital storage.

A side scan sonar system consists of a topside processing unit, a cable for electronic transmission and towing, and a towfish. Costs can vary greatly depending on the system, the options and the technology.

The typical data output consists of a classic gray scale paper chart recorder that can be computerized to apply a variety of false colours to certain signal strengths. The signal will vary depending whether the beam bounces off a hard rock or soft sand and mud. The most important features are indicated through the height of the "shadows" created by objects rising above the seafloor. They provide a three-dimensional quality to the record, and the height of an object can be easily calculated

A member of a boat crew prepares to deploy a Klein 3000 side scan sonar towfish. (Image courtesy of Garry Kozak/Klein Associates)

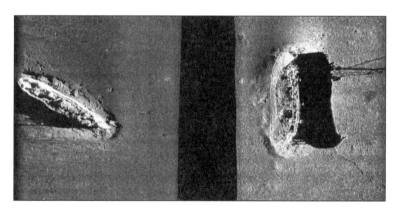

Klein 3000 side scan sonar shipwreck images.
Note the scouring effect around the image on the left, indicating a strong bottom current. The shadow along the image on the right indicates the height of the wreck off the seabed.
(Image courtesy of Garry Kozak/Klein Associates)

A Klein 3000 side scan sonar image of the SS *Portland* off the coast of Massachusetts. A sidewheel steamer of 291 feet, the *Portland* sank November 26,1898, after leaving Boston just as a blizzard bore down on the New England seaboard.
(Image courtesy of Garry Kozak/Klein Associates)

from the right triangle created by the beam angle, seafloor and target shadow. The intensity of shadows also tells us something about the makeup of the object. Acoustically opaque objects will have a lighter shadow.

The towfish generates one pulse of energy at a time and waits for the sound to be reflected back. The imaging range is determined by how long the towfish waits before transmitting the next pulse of acoustic energy. The image is developed one line of data at a time. Hard objects reflect more energy, causing a dark signal on the image; soft objects that do not reflect energy as well show up as lighter signals. The absence of sound, such as shadows behind objects, shows up as white areas on a sonar image. Search patterns are usually run as a series of parallel lines that ensure overlapping coverage of the side scan sonar.

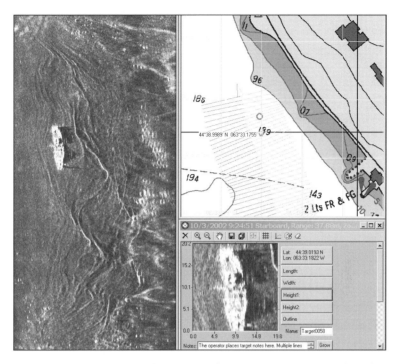

A side scan sonar image of an unidentified ship on the bottom of Halifax
Harbour. It may be a hospital ferry that sank in the 1920s.
(Image courtesy of Garry Kozak/Klein Associates)

Under certain circumstances 200 percent coverage is obtained by
running a second search pattern perpendicular to the first over
the same area.

The cost of mounting a search using this technology can be
very expensive, especially when using state-of-the-art digital technology, but the potential rewards can sometimes far outweigh the
risks. In many cases they can stagger the imagination.

12

Scuba Tourism Opportunities

To many recreational divers who travel to the Caribbean or the South Pacific on a regular basis, the mere mention of Canada ignites images of polar bears and igloos. Add the words Nova Scotia and those images change to an unexplored and undiscovered part of Canada's rugged east coast. Many global travellers refer to Nova Scotia as the land of ten months winter and two months poor skating.

But to a great many discriminating wreck divers from central and western Canada, the United Kingdom, and the northeast U.S.A., Nova Scotia has long been one of the best kept secrets in the scuba tourism industry. Nova Scotia incidentally has the highest concentration of recorded shipwrecks in the Northern Hemisphere, a staggering ten thousand documented shipwrecks. What's even more astounding is the fact that less than five percent of these wrecks have ever been located. The potential for discovery and exploration of new shipwreck sites is unlimited.

The dive season in Nova Scotia starts in May and can run well into October. Water temperatures will vary from 30° Fahrenheit in May to 60° Fahrenheit in July. The underwater visibility on the east coast averages twenty to thirty feet on a bad day and up to sixty feet plus on good days. Combine these facts with the

Scuba diving tourists can bring an economic injection to coastal communities. From left to right are Harry Dort, Stephanie Hillson, Terry Dwyer, Andy Olson, Robert Guertin, Ally Wynn, and Suzi Watters (kneeling). (Photo by Norbert Duckworth)

current exchange rate on the Canadian dollar and you have the makings of a new, extremely economical and sustainable scuba tourism industry.

The Nova Scotia Tourism Division of the Department of Tourism, Culture and Heritage refers to scuba tourism as "Nova Scotia's newest, most lucrative and mushrooming Adventure Tourism." Adventure travel is one of the world's fastest growing tourism sectors. At the Canadian Tourism Commission, analysts believe that the worldwide demand for adventure vacations will continue to grow, pushing these sector revenues higher every year.

The recently released *Nova Scotia Marine Tourism Study*, prepared for the provincial government by the Economic Planning Group of Canada, ranked Scuba Diving as number one of the top five marine tourism markets identified for Nova Scotia. The study observed: "It is an opportunity for Nova Scotia to promote a world class product among a much targeted user group." The report also recommended that further development be done on the scuba diving product. Scuba tourism offers the participant all the necessary ingredients that adventure travel has to offer: excitement, a level of risk, unique experiences, education, and fun. It does, however, require that a certain infrastructure of services and products be in place to cater to visiting divers.

Shipwrecks are non-renewable resources, while scuba diving is an adventure sport that is equipment intensive and requires certain prerequisite skills and training. Local adventure tourism operators are just beginning to scratch the surface of this lucrative, growing market.

To demonstrate the market potential, consider these facts and figures. The United Kingdom and the northeastern United States are only two examples of vast untapped markets for scuba tourism. The U.K. is, without question, the single largest cold-water scuba market in the world with over 150,000 recreational sport divers. The northeastern U.S. has more than 50,000 recreational sport divers.

These divers will travel in groups of eight to sixteen divers at a time and they will stay for eight to fourteen days per visit. The typical dive season for Nova Scotia is May to October, six months or twenty-four weeks. The economic and financial benefits for seasonal small businesses, sustainable employment and tourism related businesses in Nova Scotia's coastal communities are staggering.

A typical group of divers will require the following products and services:

> – dive boats (1 to 2 boats a day for 8 to 14 days)
> – accommodations (8 to 16 cottages, cabins or rooms per day for 8 to 14 days)
> – rental vehicles (2 to 3 vehicles per day for 8 to 14 days)
> – meals and beverages (24 to 48 meals per day for 8 to 14 days)
> – souvenir purchases, shopping and visits to various local attractions in the area.

For many of Nova Scotia's coastal communities, this exciting new tourism sector is ripe for the picking. Specifically, communities in Yarmouth, Queens, Guysborough, and Victoria Counties have an unlimited and untapped potential for scuba tourism possibilities. These coastal communities, and others in places like Newfoundland, simply need to get involved – to start marketing themselves and begin building an infrastructure necessary to attract and retain scuba divers from all over the world.

Many of the coastal communities that already have an abundance of shipwrecks should be encouraged to research, locate and document them. There are vast sources of untapped income and revenue that can be derived from this unique type of adventure tourism. It is my opinion that scuba tourism and marine-based tourism is the future for many coastal communities here in Nova Scotia.

Shipwrecks symbolize different things to different people and are viewed by many as an enigma. On one hand, they are a tragedy, often associated with suffering, loss of life and, in some cases like the *Arrow*, horrible environmental damage. But shipwrecks that were once seen as catastrophes have now become a wonderful boon to the environment, providing a base for a rich marine ecosystem and a magnet for scuba diving tourism.

13

Scuba Diving: The Ultimate Adventure

If you want to explore or visit an actual shipwreck in its natural surroundings, you will need to buy an ROV or learn how to scuba dive. Learning to scuba dive means enrolling in a recognized open water scuba course. I have included this chapter on scuba courses to acquaint the readers who are not certified divers, but might like to become divers, with this exciting and fun recreation. Without a doubt, scuba diving is the fastest growing adventure sport in the world. When it comes to fun and fitness, scuba diving leads the pack and it is enjoyed by people of all ages. As a sport, scuba diving is unique because it has no age limitations, it's non-competitive, and best of all it's a sport that you can travel with. Most anyone in good health and who is physically fit can learn to scuba dive. For those of you in search of some adventure, some relaxation or just something different, scuba diving is for you.

Anyone thinking about scuba diving should consider first trying it in a pool, under the supervision of a qualified scuba instructor. This is what is commonly referred to as an Introductory Scuba Lesson or a Discover Scuba Experience. Any one of these is a most enjoyable and rewarding experience. Once you have taken the first step of trying scuba diving in a pool, and have experienced "breathing underwater" and the feeling of "weightlessness" you will be ready to enroll in an accredited Open Water Scuba Course. There are many international certifying agencies to choose from that offer this type of training: Scuba Schools International (SSI), Professional Association of Diving Instructors (PADI), National Association of Underwater Instructors (NAUI), and American Canadian Underwater Certification (ACUC), to name a few.

A scuba course is your ticket to a lifetime of intense adventure. Learning to scuba dive is safe, affordable and requires a modest amount of training. An average entry-level certification course takes approximately forty hours to complete during daytime or evening classes conducted over two full weekends or over several weeks. In order to earn a scuba certification, you will participate in classroom sessions and practice essential diving skills in a pool. Finally, your knowledge will be tested on a written exam and then you get to apply your skills during four or five open water training dives in the ocean.

After successfully completing a program, you will have earned the Open Water Diver Certification card. At present, this card is your ticket to local diving, equipment rentals and purchases, as well as opportunities to expand your diving skills through advanced and specialty dive programs. Once you have completed your course and received your certification, the world's oceans are your playground.

For those who travel, rest assured that not only is your certification internationally recognized, but because you trained in the cold Atlantic Ocean here in Nova Scotia, you and your certification will be well-respected wherever you travel in the world. The opportunities are endless. For other types of diving you will need additional training. Dive trips to the Caribbean are often arranged by various scuba clubs and travel organizations. You may, after obtaining some experience, also decide to arrange your own trip with some friends.

Scuba diving allows you to become part of a beautiful and mysterious world. As a visitor, you will be able to meet some of its residents, see some of its wonders and learn some of its secrets. The next step is up to you.

Please keep in mind that once you become a certified open water diver, this is only the beginning, a license to learn, if you will. To continue your adventures in diving and before you embark on your first boat dive, you should take an Advanced Open Water Diver Course, as this will help prepare you and make your first experience a positive one. For some types of diving you will need additional training. In the constantly changing sport of scuba diving, continuing education is the key to unlocking many doors. Specialty courses will provide you with the necessary experience, training and education to safely enjoy and experience some new adventures in diving.

There is a common misconception that an Advanced Diver Course makes you an "advanced diver." This is not the case. An Advanced Diver Course is a stepping stone on your journey of learning. You actually become an advanced diver in the true sense of the words by continuing your diving education, which means enrolling in a variety of different specialty courses and by diving frequently (this refers to logged dives in your personal log book) on a regular basis and in different types of conditions. For example, an Advanced Open Water Diver Course is an introduction to specialty diving and can be a useful way to expand basic diving skills and experience.

Specialty courses – such as underwater photography, underwater video, night diving, shipwreck diving, boat diving, etc. – will add a whole new dimension to scuba diving. The more varied your skills and experiences, the more likely it is that you will never be bored with the sport of scuba diving.

Each diving area is unique. Wherever you dive, remember to plan and prepare to climatize yourself to the local conditions in the areas you are planning to visit. No matter where you dive, investigate local conditions first.

After twenty-three years in the recreational diving industry I would like offer the would-be diver a few valuable nuggets of advice.

While many people complete a scuba course and become certified scuba divers in a week or less, there is no strict time limit in which the course must be completed. A minimum of five training days should be allowed for completion. Some dive shops conduct their courses in a regimented, impersonal and "mechanical" manner, often resulting in reduced quality of training, no fun and an overall negative experience.

If you want to maximize your training and enjoyment you should select a private or semi-private scuba course. A private (one or two people) or a semi-private (three to four people) course means a lot more personal attention and more personal in-water time to practice and develop skills. Private courses are very flexible and are tailored to fit your personal or professional schedule. You should also get to schedule the specific dates and times. The end result is a more confident and better trained diver. These fun, self-paced sessions make it easy to complete the course without the hassle of tight schedules and no penalties for missed classes. Home study CD Roms, in video or DVD format, means less time in the classroom. No pressure. No wasted time. No strict schedules to meet. It's easy and you can start whenever you like.

A wise old scuba instructor once told me, "Many receive advice but only the wise profit from it." So shop around, compare the details and do some thorough research. You will be glad you did and you will most assuredly get greater value for your time and money by investing in a private or semi-private course. They range anywhere from $500 to $700 per person. Ask lots of questions about the experience of the instructor and ask specifically about what is and what is not included in the course. Make it a point to ask for references or referrals from past customers and students.

Not all scuba courses are the same. Prices will vary, as will the length of the course, the course materials and the course content. There are many reasons why this is so, but in the end it boils down to pure economics. Are you familiar with the expression "time and money"? The difference between a $299 group rate course and a $599 private course is "time and money" – yours to be exact.

I cannot overstate how important actual scuba course materials are. The more materials you have to learn from, the more you will get out of the course. I highly recommend that your standard course materials should include a choice of a set of video tapes, a CD Rom or a DVD (for home study, future reference and refresher training), a manual, a set of plastic dive tables, a professional organizer, and a logbook.

Most dive stores require that you purchase or supply your own "scuba grade" mask, snorkel, fins and boots. This is a normal practice; because of sizing issues it is not possible to carry a rental inventory to fit all sizes and shapes of people. But don't get talked into an inexpensive discount kit. When it comes to buying scuba equipment – just like scuba courses – you get very much what you pay for, so please take the time to do some research. Let me share a very common and well used expression among professional divers: "The bitterness of poor quality remains long after the sweetness of low price is forgotten."

This is the best advice I can offer you: fit, comfort and quality should be the three deciding factors on any equipment purchase. When it comes to diving equipment, I would like to impart yet another nugget of information. The market place is saturated with generic knock-off brands that are not comparable to brand name scuba equipment. Stick to brand name equipment; it costs a little more, but it is well worth the initial investment. Having your own personal equipment will make your course that much more enjoyable, and it will enhance your overall experience.

14

Boat Diving in Nova Scotia

If you are in search of adventure, some relaxation or just something different, you should try scuba diving from a boat. Most
shipwreck sites here in Nova Scotia are often too far away for
shore access. Boat diving offers you unlimited access to some of
the best shipwreck sites in Nova Scotia. Boat diving increases
your fun time, your bottom time and it reduces the effort and
problems that are often associated with shore diving, such as
traffic, parking, long walks with gear and/or long surface swims.

Whether you are diving from a rugged Zodiac or a Bombard
inflatable or one of Nova Scotia's famous Cape Island fishing
boats, boat diving is the only way to visit and explore the
best shipwrecks Nova Scotia has to offer. I have included this
chapter to make the reader aware of the many basic practices
and techniques that will ultimately enhance their boat diving
experience. The following information and suggestions are just
that; they are not a substitute for experience. Every diver interested
in shipwrecks should continue their education with an Advanced
Scuba Course, a Boat Diver Specialty Course and a Wreck
Diver Specialty Course. These courses will supply you not only
with necessary information, but with actual dives and real time
experience.

Rule Number One: always plan ahead. It has been said that wars have been won and lost based on planning. The same holds true for boat diving. You should always choose an itinerary and a dive boat that provides the types of diving you are seeking and matches the training and experience you currently have. Once you decide, be prepared to spend some time on a boat. An average two-tank boat dive in Halifax Harbour can last as long four to five hours, while a day trip to St. Paul Island can last up to twelve hours. If you think you might get seasick easily, consider taking an over-the-counter remedy prior to boarding the boat. Once you start to feel seasick it's too late for medication to do you any good.

You should always adjust your diet the night before to be more motion tolerant by eliminating spicy and greasy foods. Drink more water than usual. It is important to be well hydrated and most people don't drink enough plain water on a daily basis. Remember, when you are outside in the wind or scuba diving and breathing dry air, your body needs extra water replenishment. Water is much better than pop for hydration.

Bring lots of clothes and a hat so you have a choice to stay warm or cool. If you do start to feel queasy, try to find a place on the boat with fresh air and where you can focus on a distant horizon. Stay low and near the boat's centre. Low and centre reduces the amount of movement and the horizon gives visual clues to help your other senses find equilibrium. If you get seasick, please do it over the downwind side of the boat. Don't go below deck or inside the boat.

Equipment Planning

Before you leave home or the dive shop, make sure that you have "action packed" your dive bag. How to "action pack" changes with the type of diving you plan to do, but the concept is to put the things you will use first on the top of the bag and the items you will use last at the bottom of the bag. For example, the first piece of equipment you will use is your buoyancy compensator, to attach to your tank. Next you might attach your pony bottle (if you have one) then your regulator(s). You get the picture.

The object is to never remove a piece of equipment from the bag until you are ready to put it in place or use it. The same principle applies in reverse: when you take it off, put it in the bag. Your companions sharing limited deck space will appreciate your dressing in and out of the gear bag, plus you have less of a chance of losing or breaking equipment. You should also mark your personal dive equipment with a dot of paint, a piece of coloured tape or your initials. It reduces loss, accidental mix-ups and thefts. Always remember to bring a spares kit – extra fin and mask straps, etc. There is nothing more frustrating and embarrassing than being anchored over a wreck site, putting your fins on and breaking a strap, then finding out that your dive buddy does not have a spare.

Dive Boat Courtesy and Etiquette

Boats pitch and roll constantly, especially at anchor. If you leave a tank standing on the deck, it will fall over, injuring a diver or breaking something – guaranteed. Always put a tank on its side or fasten it in a rack whenever you take your hands away from it. It is also a law of nature that if you sit on a boat deck to don your tank, your head will be at the exact same height as a standing diver wearing a tank and you will get smacked. Sit on a bench or the pontoon of the Zodiac to don your tank and have your buddy lift it to assist you.

The macho throw-it-over-your-head donning is an accident waiting to happen, and it is an outdated skill as well. When you gear up, don everything but your mask, snorkel and fins. Always do a buddy check – check out each other's gear configuration for safety – and then move towards the exit point with the remainder of your equipment in your hand. Use the mask rinsing bucket (if one is available); don your mask, then your fins at the exit point.

Don't try to walk around wearing fins on an unstable boat. Try not to clog the exit area as other people may be waiting and should not have to stand by while you make last minute changes. These should be done before approaching the exit.

The Entry

Anchoring a boat is not like parking a car. Boats don't stay in one place – they tend to swing on their anchors. The bigger the surface area of the wheel house and the stronger the wind, the more the boat will swing back and forth. It will travel in an arc, pivoting from the anchor. The longer the anchor line, the bigger the area of movement. Before you leap into the water, tune into the boat's movement. As it swings back and forth like a pendulum, you should be planning your entry. Jump when the boat is moving away from your entry point, not when it is about to pass over it. If there is a specific spot you want to dive, jump when you are on that side of the arc rather than waiting until you must swim all the way back. When diving from a large charter boat, with a lot of scope on the anchor line, the distance from one side of the swing arc to the other might be a ten-minute swim.

Before you leap always look down into the water. Is anyone just below the surface? Look at your feet one last time. Are your fins on? Don't laugh; everyone jumps in sometime without their fins and sometimes even without their weight belt. Once in the water, move away from the entry area; either make a surface dive and descend well clear of the area or surface swim towards the anchor line. If you have a hard time clearing your ears, use the anchor line as a guide to descend feetfirst, constantly clearing your ears slowly as you descend.

In poor visibility the anchor line provides a visual frame of reference that reduces the chance of vertigo. Remember that the anchor line stretches and relaxes as waves pass under the boat, so don't be surprised when it moves. When your dive is over, you should always plan to finish your dive at the anchor and ascend using the anchor line. If your dive plan allows for a direct ascent, watch and listen for the boat, so it does not swing on top of you at the surface. Many dive boats trail a current line behind the boat in case you surface down current. This line typically has a

Captain Albert Leahey (left) and scuba instructor Harvey Morash assist
divers coming onboard. Divemaster Jennifer Millet supervises.
(Photo by Terry Dwyer)

large bright buoy on the end, making it easier to spot. It swings
with the boat, so assess which direction the boat is swinging,
how fast you are moving in the surface current and whether you
can wait for the current line to float over to your location.

If you can't wait, then swim to the line. Once you grab
hold of the line you should stop kicking, catch your breath and
use your arm strength to pull yourself back to the boat. Pull
hand over hand, using short reaches as you glide over the line.
Remember if you try to kick, your legs will get tangled in the
line. If you are too tired to do this, an observant divemaster or
one of the crew will recognize this and pull you in.

The Exit

Once you are back to the boat, boarding techniques will then
have to be assessed. Stop a little way from the boarding ladder or
swim platform and check out the conditions. Is the boat plung-
ing up and down? You could get hit by the ladder or the swim

platform. In this situation, you time your approach so that when the ladder or platform goes down in the water, you quickly swim on to it. You need to be firmly on the ladder or platform when it begins its trip up and out of the water. Hand all extra gear to the crew members or clip it to lines that are pre-hung over the side.

There is no need to climb a ladder carrying camera or video equipment. If the water is calm, the divemaster will have you hang onto the ladder or platform, remove your fins and pass them up to a crew member, then climb up the ladder. If there is any surface current or you are afraid that you might not make it up the ladder, you may want to thread your fins on your forearms, keeping them available in case you fall back in the water.

While we are on the topic of falling back into the water, it really does happen, so please don't crowd beneath the ladder or platform because some day you will get hit by a falling diver or a tank that comes tumbling down. Always let the person ahead of you clear the exit area before you get in line directly under or behind them.

If the boat has a wide platform, wait until it is at its lowest point in the water, then swim as far up on the platform as you can. Pull your knees underneath you and hold on for the upward ride. Stand up only after you have stabilized your position. Try and avoid rolling on your side. You can actually stay in the kneeling position through a lot of rocking and rolling and not fall off the platform.

Once you are back on the boat, take your tank off and secure it. Take off the regulator so no one accidentally thinks it is a full tank and ready to use. Undress into your gear bag so it is action packed for your next dive. If you have handed any fins or other gear to the crew, claim it promptly. This avoids any mix ups and chaos when you dress for the next dive. When your clean-up chores are done, log your dive (this is very important as it provides proof of experience) and enjoy the special time after the dive: that exhilarating high and a feeling of contentment after an adventure. When you are ready to depart the dive boat, do a thorough search to make sure you are not forgetting anything. Please assist in the offloading of all equipment – many

Our two L'Auguste project boats, included a 16 foot Zodiac Pro RIB and a 24 foot Bombard Explorer. Both style boats are very reliable, robust, versatile and useful on any ship wreck project.

hands make light work. Remember the hardworking captain and or crew. If you appreciated their services remember to say thank you. Diving from a boat adds a whole new dimension to scuba diving.

Diving from a Zodiac

Here in Nova Scotia, inflatable boats like Zodiac and Bombard have become the most popular and trusted boats for diving, especially open ocean diving. The Zodiac, made famous by Jacques Cousteau's television specials, stands out as the most recognized and preferred inflatable in the world. Diving from a Zodiac is one of the most enjoyable, easy and rewarding types of diving. With a small Zodiac you can get away from the crowds to dive secret spots that most people will never get the chance to dive.

Zodiac and Bombard inflatable boats have several advantages over other small boats you might think of diving from. These boats range in size from ten feet to twenty-four feet. For diving purposes a fourteen- or sixteen-foot inflatable with a 40-horse-power Yamaha engine will easily cruise with four divers and their equipment.

For a business or dive charter operation a larger 19- or 24-foot Zodiac or Bombard will accommodate six to eight divers quite comfortably. Unlike the Cape Island style fishing boats, an inflatable can be trailered to just about any location where there is a small boat ramp/launch. Inflatables have a shallow draft and they're lightweight, making them very responsive and easy to operate. They have separate air chambers that distribute their buoyancy around the sides in the inflated sections, making them incredibly stable and seaworthy. Because of their stability a fully equipped diver or even two can sit on one side of the inflatable with little concern for capsizing or swamping. Finally, because they are inflated, these boats will handle more load than the same size conventional boats. For their size and capacity, inflatables cost less than the same size conventional boat and their upkeep is low. You can spend a lot on an inflatable if you want to, but you can also be economical and still have a versatile craft. Zodiacs and Bombards are cost effective, reliable dive boats that are a lot of fun and easy to dive from.

I personally have owned several Zodiacs over the past ten years. Today I own a 16-foot C-5 Bombard Commando inflatable, and my dive company owns and operates a 24-foot RIB (Rigid Inflatable Boat) Zodiac SRMN 730 (SRMN is an acronym for Sea Rib Military Navy) with twin four-stroke Yamaha 100-horsepower engines. Both boats are trailerized and can be transported anywhere in Nova Scotia.

When it comes to outboard motors, my choice has always been Yamaha. I have been using four-stroke Yamaha products for many years and, in my opinion, they are without question the most trouble-free, quiet, fuel-efficient and reliable outboard engines on the market today. On more than one occasion I have found myself in some very unpleasant weather and sea conditions over the past few years and I have never hesitated to shut down and restart my Yamaha engines, ever. Over the years I have put thousands of hours on my Yamaha engines in all seasons, in all temperatures and in all types of weather and I can tell you, when the chips are down, and you find yourself twenty miles from the mainland in a raging storm, you had better be prepared and you had better be confident in your outboard engine.

15

Aids to Navigation

Early mariners pioneered navigation technology, using the stars to safely sail in search of adventure. These days marine adventurers of every kind, especially wreck hunters, look to the constellation of Global Positioning System (GPS) satellites to know precisely where they are and where they are going. Accurate navigation is vital when travelling on open waters and since most shipwreck sites are generally difficult to locate and relocate at the best of times, you will need access to some form of aid to navigation and positioning equipment.

Navigation equipment is very much like diving equipment – you get what you pay for. It is necessary to have this equipment with you if you intend to locate or relocate a specific wreck site. Marine electronics like a chart plotter, radar, depth sounder and a GPS are easy to use and very affordable to buy. In this chapter the reader can gain a better perspective on and understanding of how easy it is to use this type of modern navigation equipment.

The Global Positioning System

The Global Positioning System (GPS) is a constellation of satellites which orbit the earth, transmitting precise time and position (latitude, longitude and altitude) information. With a GPS receiver, users can determine their location anywhere on earth. Position and navigation information is vital to a broad range of professional and personal activities, including boating, surveying, aviation, national defense, vehicle tracking, navigation, and more. The complete system consists of twenty-four satellites orbiting about twelve thousand miles above the earth, and five ground stations to monitor and manage the satellite constellation. These satellites provide 24-hour-a-day coverage for both two- and three-dimensional positioning anywhere on earth.

Development of the $10-billion GPS satellite navigation system was begun in the 1970s by the U.S. Department of Defense, which continues to manage the system, to provide continuous, world-wide positioning and navigation data to U.S. military forces around the globe. However, GPS has an even broader civilian, commercial application. To meet these needs, GPS offers two levels of service, one for civilian access and the second encrypted for exclusive military use. The GPS signals are available to an unlimited number of users simultaneously.

How Does GPS Work?

The basis of GPS technology is precise time and position information. Using atomic clocks (accurate to within a second every seventy thousand years) and location data, each satellite continuously broadcasts the time and its position. A GPS receiver receives these signals, listening to three or more satellites at once, to determine the user's position on earth. By measuring the time interval between the transmission and the reception of the satellite signal, the GPS receiver calculates the distance between the user and the satellite. Using the distance measurements of at least three satellites in an algorithm computation, the GPS receiver arrives at an accurate position fix.

For example, the position information on my chart plotter GPS receiver may be displayed as longitude/latitude, Universal Transverse Mercator, Military Grid or other system coordinates. Information must be received from three satellites in order to obtain two-dimensional (longitude and latitude) fixes, and four satellites are required for three-dimensional (latitude, longitude and altitude) positioning.

Each satellite continuously broadcasts two signals, L1 and L2. The L1 frequency contains the C/A code which provides Standard Positioning Service (SPS) for worldwide civilian use. The encrypted P code is broadcast on both the L1 and L2 frequency, resulting in the Precise Positioning Service (PPS) for military use. The SPS signal will provide a civilian user an accuracy of better than twenty-five metres. Because they are so accurate, civilian GPS receivers using the SPS signal are sometimes subjected to Selective Availability (SA) interference by the United States Government to maintain optimum military effectiveness of the system.

When engaged, SA inserts random errors in the data transmitted by the satellites. As a result, SPS signal accuracy can be reduced to a hundred metres. However, using a technique called differential GPS (DGPS), the user can overcome the effect of SA interference and increase the overall accuracy of the GPS receiver. With DGPS, one receiver unit is placed at a known location and the position information from that receiver is used to calculate corrections in the position data transmitted by the satellites. The corrected information is then transmitted to other GPS receivers in the area. The resulting real time accuracy is in the ten-metre range. Sub-metre accuracy can be obtained by using DGPS and post processing calculations in static positioning.

My point for including the above explanation of how GPS works is twofold. First of all and as previously stated, in order to locate or return to a shipwreck site, you will need some type of positioning equipment. Since it is well documented that GPS is more accurate than Loran numbers, I highly recommend using a chart plotter with a built-in GPS. Secondly, the price of purchasing a chart plotter or a GPS unit has come down significantly, thereby making it more affordable for the average recreational diver or boat owner to own one. These products also make boating and shipwreck hunting safer, easier and more enjoyable experiences

Next to choosing the boat itself, the choice of navigation equipment is one of the most important decisions that the boat owner/operator will have to make. There are many different products and some new exciting technologies to choose from, and there are prices to suit just about everyone's budget.

16

Underwater Video

These days most people own a video camera of some type. Why not take it with you on a dive and bring back some great memories? You will be amazed at how easy it is to shoot your first underwater video. You don't need to understand photography or complex electronics to enjoy it. You only need to set a few simple switches when you place the video camera inside a waterproof housing. Underwater you simply aim the camera at your subject and press the record button. When you see your first underwater video tape you will relive all the high points of the dive. You will see your buddy swimming over a shipwreck and you will enjoy the action and the excitement. Your first efforts will be exciting; it will not matter how well you handled the camera. Underwater video housings are affordable and very user friendly, and there is an excellent selection of books and magazines available that specifically deal with underwater video and photography. Make it a habit to read up on the system and reread the owner's manual several times, highlighting the various important information and suggestions.

The most important aspect of shooting underwater video and diving in general is buoyancy control. Avoid disturbing the bottom silt and try not to come in contact with anything on

179

the seabed. Work on controlling your breathing and your buoyancy. Your video will be much more appealing. Remember, you are trying to make yourself a steady shooting platform. The less movement you make the better your video will be. Work on attaining a comfort zone underwater. The more comfortable you are underwater, the more controlled your breathing will be and the steadier your video will be.

Remember to take extra special care with the storage, packing, unpacking, shipping and transporting of your camera equipment, even more so than your personal diving equipment. Camera equipment is not nearly as rugged as diving equipment. You should be very cognizant of using, handling and storing camera equipment on boats, because of the limited space and the amount of equipment and people onboard. You can also "action pack" your camera gear and plan ahead for the type of shooting you will be doing.

This means the actual preparation of the system prior to using it in the field, mounting the ballast bars, light arms and other attachments. It also includes prepping the housing, checking and cleaning the lens and then the actual camera set up, including things like the focus, wide angle, lens attachments, etc. The very last thing to do before you enter the water is a systems check, stand by-record check and a focus check. The following check list will help.

Before Your Dive

1. Inventory, assemble and test everything ahead of time. Make a complete list, taking into account all your planned activities which may require specialized equipment. (e.g., patch video cables, screws and attachments from disassembled components).

2. Check the condition of the nickel-cadmium power cells (Ni-Cad batteries) used in camera and lighting systems. Always deplete the batteries after every dive by continually depressing rewind and fast forward. Deplete the video lights by submerging them in cold water and turning them on, then off till the batter-

Amphibico Underwater Imaging Equipment Inc., Montreal, Canada designs and manufactures the most reliable and highest quality underwater video housing in the world.

ies are spent. Recharge all your batteries to manufacturer's specifications.

3.   Replace all disposable batteries and always carry spares. Clean all battery contacts in systems with a pencil eraser to remove oxides.

4.   Mark all tapes and cassettes clearly with your name and telephone number and always date your batteries, tapes, notes, etc. Also mark removable items (lens caps, etc.) to prevent a mix up with another photographer's equipment.

5.   Attach a white tape label to all camera and lighting systems. Write instructions for reference for focus, white balance, shutter speed, charge times, etc.

Pre-Dive Precautions

1.   Before diving if possible, submerge the empty camera housing in water to check for leaks.

2.   Before installing the camera in the housing, check all camera settings, zoom, focus and white balance.

3.   Seal the camera in the housing *before* leaving an air-conditioned room to prevent internal condensation.

Shooting Tips

1.   Have your buoyancy control down to a science, check weight and balance, equipment fit, etc. before diving with a camera.

2.   If an exciting or rare specimen is seen before the dive, start the camera before entering the water and edit later.

3.   Check and clean the lens of bubbles once you are in the water and periodically during the dive.

4.   Depending on your goals, several short (5- to 7-second) shots are more effective than long (20- to 30-second) shots.

5.   Hold the camera steady. Get a comfortable grip; balance the housing with small weights if necessary.

6.   Minimize panning and tilting. Instead move the camera slowly.

7.   Always point and shoot down or across. Never point up into the haze in the water column unless you have a subject to film.

8.   Let the subject swim through the shot. Do not follow movements with the camera.

9.   Think of a logical sequence for your shot and develop a shot list. Avoid an unrelated series of video snapshots.

10.   For natural light shots at twenty feet or deeper, use a UR Pro filter to enhance colours. Use the Daylight Colour balance setting on the camera.

11.   For close-ups with a light, remove the UR Pro filter and set the camera to Indoor Colour Balance.

12.   Check shutter speed. If you are diving in deep dark water use 1/60th. For upward silhouettes (toward the sun) use 1/200th or more to avoid image burn out.

13.   Fill the viewfinder/monitor with the subject. Avoid long shots and when you focus underwater, make sure to refocus back out or everything will be out of focus for the rest of the dive.

14.   Shoot important scenes twice; you can edit later.

15.   Go easy on the camera controls; avoid playing with zoom. Keep the operations as simple as possible.

16.   The best results will be obtained with natural light if the sun is directly overhead during calm water periods.

17.   Placing the sun behind your shoulder during shooting will produce the best colours.

18.   Wide angle is the preferred focus setting for best results with a subject, as close as possible to the housing. This will reduce the water column and the amount of particulate between subject and lens.

19.   Zooming in and out during shooting is not recommended unless absolutely necessary as telephoto will magnify particulates. Swimming towards the subject is a much more visually pleasing filming method.

20.   Use image stabilizer if available on your camera when filming macro to minimize camera movement during high magnification. Image stabilizer is not as critical while using wide angle and will only use battery power unnecessarily.

21.   In low light situations, add light with optional video lights for brighter and more vibrant colours. As light level falls so does colour saturation. Lights will also provide necessary fill during daylight shooting. If this technique is used, filtration of light using a colour correction filter will be necessary for accurate colour rendition.

After the Dive

Service and clean your equipment as soon as possible after the dive. Recharge batteries. I also highly recommend soaking the housing and lights overnight in fresh water SALTX solution mix. Remove all screws and loosen all ball joint fittings to ensure a complete flush with fresh water. The next day it should then be dried, disassembled, cleaned and repacked or stored for the next dive. Never store your housing in sealed cases in direct sunlight as extreme heat can be generated in these conditions and can damage certain internal components of the housing.

17

Deep Star Exploration

One of my favourite mentors once told me that unless you try to do something beyond what you have already mastered, you will never grow. So in the summer of 2001 I decided to enter the shipwreck exploration business. It was something I had always wanted to do. I felt that I had enough diving experience and acquired shipwreck knowledge, that it was now or never. I pored over my twenty years of shipwreck research information and selected what I felt would make the most desirable projects. I contacted some former associates, many of whom were retired treasure hunters and salvage divers. They offered to assist me with their knowledge and experience.

The pieces of the puzzle were slowly starting to come together. I came up with a list of specific areas off the coast of Cape Breton that I felt contained the remains of valuable shipwrecks. On August 8, 2002, I contacted the Registrar of Mines and Claims at the Department on Natural Resources in Halifax and made application for several different Treasure Trove Licenses around Cape Breton Island. On September 23, 2002, I filed the necessary work proposals with the Department of Natural Resources, as is required by the department. That same day, I also made several applications to the Nova Scotia Museum of

Natural History for the Heritage Research Reconnaissance Permits (which are necessary and required for Treasure Trove applications).

The Heritage Research Reconnaissance Permits were granted within weeks. The Treasure Trove Licenses took quite a bit longer. Because of unforeseen changes in the government which included the Minister of Natural Resources actually losing his seat in an election, the applications simply got caught in a lengthy bureaucracy and the licenses were not issued until 2004.

While all this paper work was happening, John Schumacherapproached me indicating that he wanted to get back into the business. I welcomed the news and John as an active associate. John was one of the original divers who discovered part of the *Auguste* wreck in 1977.

John felt strongly that the stern section of the *Auguste* wreck was further outside of where the current salvage was being conducted. In his opinion the stern contained the vast majority of treasure. John had a theory that over the past twenty-six years there was never any jewelry or large amounts of gold coins recovered. It was well documented the *Auguste* was carrying seven very wealthy ladies who had onboard all their wealth, yet no jewelry was ever found. St. Luc de la Corne and his brother were two of the wealthiest people in North America at the time of their deportation, and they too had all their worldly possessions onboard. John felt that if and when the stern section was found it would all be in one area. Given that there were never any actual pieces of the stern section of the ship recovered, he could very well be right.

On August 15, 2003, John Schumacher filed a Treasure Trove application to the Department of Natural Recourses, requesting the outside perimeter of the original 1977-78 grid. His grid extended one mile out from the original grid and eight miles across on all sides, in effect boxing in the original grid. To our complete and utter astonishment the Auguste Expedition Company had not secured this area.

Once it became known that John and I had actually formed a treasure hunting company and were actively seeking investors to finance our search, other rival treasure hunters came out of the woodwork and tried to intimidate us, deter us and even discredit us with potential investors, locally and internationally.

We were not intimidated nor were we deterred, and eventually we were granted the three-year treasure trove license for the outside perimeter of the *Auguste* site. We were also granted several more licenses for other valuable areas around Cape Breton Island, including St. Paul Island and Cape St. Esprit. In February 2004 we formed Deep Star Exploration Inc. with the sole objective to search for, document and recover "treasure trove" from shipwrecks.

While I was waiting for the licenses to be issued, I went about creating a detailed business plan that would contain enough information to whet the appetite of any serous investor. I contacted the Mel Fisher Group at Treasure Salvors and Odyssey Marine in Florida to inquire about how they raised money. Both companies were extremely helpful and supplied me with lots of up-to-date and accurate information.

After several months of research, I assembled a five-year business plan that contains more than two hundred pages of detailed information and demonstrates how we would succeed. It covers such topics as: a confidentiality agreement; executive summary; archival research; negotiation; surveys; recovery; commercialization; marketing; sales; media spin-off operations; legal aspects of shipwreck recovery; return on investment; current technology; discoveries in waiting; Project *Auguste* Stern Section Recovery; other projects/expeditions in development; and the search team.

We certainly felt that this was an unprecedented investment opportunity and it still is; the expected return on invested capital, time or resources into our shipwreck recovery company is staggering and can be as much as five to twenty times that of the investment. An investor would also get to experience the vicarious thrill of being part of the search, part of the dream, and part of the ultimate adventure.

18

The Adventure Continues

They say that opportunities are never lost – they are just found by someone else. These two stories prove once again that truth is indeed stranger than fiction.

The first story, which came from a commercial diver, goes that back in the late 1970s a tugboat was towing a barge full of anchors and chain up the coast from Halifax to Sydney. The commercial shipping lanes are quite a way off shore. A few miles off the coast of Cape Breton the tugboat ran into very bad weather, the towline snapped and the barge broke free from the tug. Huge waves started to push the barge towards shore. The tug raced after it and succeeded in securing a line to the barge. In the process, the barge tipped and spilled all the anchors and chain. The tugboat hooked on to the barge and made for the nearest port.

A few days later after the storm subsided, the towing company contacted a commercial diving business in Halifax to send a diver to meet the tug and recover the anchors and chain. The commercial diver who was assigned the task was an oil rig diver on his way home to British Columbia from a 28-day stint on a rig. The tugboat took him to where they spilled the anchor and chain and he dropped into a hundred feet of water. When he landed on the seabed he stayed down for twenty minutes conducting a general search and then returned to the boat. No anchors and no chain. So they moved further up the coast to another location. Dive number two put him right on top of the anchors and chain. He quickly secured lines and in a matter of a few hours all was done and he was on his way back to port. Two days he was back in British Columbia.

When he got home he telephoned a commercial diver and friend of his here in Nova Scotia and told him about the job he had just completed. Then he proceeded to tell what he really saw on dive number one.

The diver from B.C. described the seabed littered with bronze cannons as far as the eye could see; visibility was excellent between seventy-five and a hundred feet. He also described a lot of material fused together and the wreck covered a very large area. Our commercial diver friend in Sydney felt strongly that this specific wreck could in fact be one of two known wrecks in that area: the *La Liberte*, which carried $500,000 in gold specie, or the *Le Triton,* which carried several millions of dollars in treasure.

This information made for a most interesting development with very exciting and real possibilities. In any case we filed that information away for a future project.

I recall being told this story sometime back in the early 1980s and I was reminded of it while applying for Treasure Trove Licenses at the Department of Natural Resources. I noted that one of our competitors had secured grids for most of the coastline and almost all the shallow water area near the Cape St. Esprit coast. But no one had yet made an application for the deep water area.

So in January 2004 John Schumacher and I contacted our-diver friend in Sydney. Through discussions we reached an agreement and he supplied us with the rough coordinates to the site, within a mile. He also agreed to come onboard the project as one of the divers. We certainly welcomed that, as he has always been considered one of the foremost authorities on shipwrecks and on salvage operations.

If we are lucky we expect to find an entire wreck together in a reasonably small area. We also expect to find a lot of perfectly preserved artifacts and parts of the ship, making the identification of the ship known fairly quickly once we locate it. Since we have not yet gone out and located this site, the story will have to be continued in volume two.

The second story came from a telephone conversation I had with an older retired gentleman in New Orleans, Louisiana. He was responding to my classified ad in *Boats and Harbors* magazine, that I had placed under Business Opportunities, looking for investors to finance the search for and recovery of treasure off the Nova Scotia coast. He asked me if I had found a ship that I will call the SS *Gold Wreck*. I indicated that I had not.

He went on to tell me that the SS *Gold Wreck* wrecked sometime in the late 1800s off the coast of Nova Scotia. She was carrying a cargo of, among other things, $400,000 in gold bullion (today it would be worth about $4 million). The gold bullion had been smuggled out of the United States during the American Civil War and was being returned (twenty-five years after the war) to its rightful owner, a wealthy family residing in Louisiana.

Her first port of call was New York, then she was bound for New Orleans. The vessel was over four hundred feet in length and had twin screws. She was owned and operated out of Hong Kong but had a Scottish connection or affiliation that allowed for a British registry. Everybody got off the vessel and the lifeboats landed near a lighthouse.

I tried to follow up with the gentleman on several occasions, as he said he had some documents relating to the loss and the insurance claim which apparently paid out $200,000 to a family member. After several calls I was informed that he and other family members had decided to "let sleeping dogs lie" and would offer no further information or assistance. End of story. So I filed this information away as another future project for our company, and hopefully I will include the rest of this story in volume two as well. Let's see what the future has in store for us.

19

Some Final Thoughts

Originally, when I started writing this book I had planned to include the GPS coordinates for every shipwreck I have personally dived on. However, over the course of the last few years, I have come to the conclusion that providing the coordinates to the wreck sites that I and a great many other divers had invested hundreds, if not thousands, of dollars and as many hours into finding was not a good idea as many divers have and will continue to incur a great deal of personal time and expense searching for shipwrecks. Most wreck hunters tend to be very secretive about their business and their successes for a number of reasons. Successful wreck hunters (amateur and professional alike) spend a lot of time and money to find unknown wrecks. Once the wreck hunter locates a wreck, they are often concerned with diving and exploring the wreck without interference from others, and this is what causes problems.

The wrecks are supposedly owned by everyone, but it does not necessarily follow that the knowledge of the wreck's location is owned by everyone. The wreck is an object while the location is knowledge that was gleaned through the personal time, energy and expense of an individual. Many people do not see the distinction between the ownership of the wreck and the ownership of its location, but it is important, because the dismissal of it fails to recognize the fundamental right of an individual to hold private intellectual property (namely the location of the wreck).

Out of mutual respect for the many wreck divers and fishermen who shared their personal knowledge and shipwreck information with me, specifically for this book, I chose not to publish the GPS coordinates or exact locations of many specific wrecks. This book was written primarily as a source of information presented in a way to encourage the reader to join in what I feel is the ultimate adventure, the search for lost shipwrecks.

Always remember to let good diving practices, common sense and courtesy prevail while you and your diving companions safely enjoy exploring the many shipwrecks here in Nova Scotia. Once again I emphasize that there is no substitute for diving experience; this can only be attained by continuing your diving education and by diving frequently and consistently.

Lastly, the ocean is a high-risk environment and it is not possible to sail or work on it without risk to life and property. Some areas present a higher risk than others. Over the years, I have learned from personal experience that the ocean can be a cruel mistress, relentless, challenging and with agendas of her own. On many a diving project we took ourselves, our diving capabilities and our company to the very edge. The ocean can also be a tremendous source of inspiration, wonder, excitement and discovery. After twenty-five years, every dive is still different and I am still excited, still learning and still experiencing new things. It's a never ending journey.

I remember my very first shipwreck dive. It was 1979 and I was fifteen years old. I remember being so captivated and mesmerized, swimming over the wreckage in Park Street Cove. That rush of excitement and the childlike sense of wonder that I experienced back in 1979 has never left me, and today I am as passionate and as enthusiastic as ever about history and about shipwrecks. I hope you have enjoyed this book and I would like to leave you with some inspirational words that I have lived my life by. Please take from them what you will: "There are many things in life that will catch your eye, but only a few will capture your heart. Pursue those." I did.

Visit the Wreck Hunter interactive website online at www.wreckhunter.ca

If you have any comments, questions or suggestions that this book or future projects, please contact me at:
shipwrecked@ns.sympatico.ca
or
P.O. Box 22133
Bayers Road RPO
Halfiax, Nova Scotia,
Canada B3L 4T7

The Wreck Hunter
Supports the Responsible Diver Program

As a responsible diver I understand and assume all the risks I may encounter while diving. My responsible diving duties include:

1. Diving within the limits of my ability and training.

2. Evaluating the conditions before every dive and making sure they fit my personal capabilities.

3. Being familiar with and checking my equipment before and during every dive.

4. Knowing my buddy's ability level as well as my own.

5. Accepting responsibility for my own safety on every dive.

The Code of the Responsible Diver

As a responsible diver . . .

I understand the risks I may encounter while diving. I will seek experience and knowledge from those with more and I will share mine with those who have less.

Superior divers . . .

use their superior knowledge to stay out of situations that would require the use of their superior skills.

Your equipment can be excellent . . .

but it is not responsible for you.

Your training can be excellent . . .

but it is not responsible for you.

Your buddy can be excellent . . .

but he or she is not responsible for you.

You are responsible for you:

be excellent.

Recommended Websites

Shipwrecks

    www.northernmaritimeresearch.com

    www.wreckhunter.net

    www.wreckhunter.ca

    www.nswrecks.net

    www.prosea.org

    www.imacdigest.com

Scatarie Island, Sambro Island, Seal Island

    www.nslps.ednet.ns.ca

St. Paul Island

    www.stpaulisland.net

    www.nslps.ednet.ns.ca

    www.wreckhunter.ca

Shipwreck Recovery Companies

    www.marexglobal.net

    www.melfisher.com

    www.shipwreck.net

Professional Numismatist/Shipwreck Coins and Artifacts
www.pngdealers.com
www.numis.co.uk

TV Programs
www.diversdowntv.com

Cyber Diver News Network
www.cdnn.info/index.html

Diving Magazines
www.divermag.com
www.wreckdivingmag.com
www.divertrainingmag.com

Diver Education and Training
www.padi.com
www.naui.org
www.acuc.ca
www.sditdi.com
www.ssiusa.com

Diving Equipment Manufacturers
www.crosscountryparts.com

Deep Sea Manned Submersibles
www.nuytco.com

Diver Propulsion Vehicles
www.farallonusa.com

Marine Magnetometers
www.marinemagnetics.com
www.deepseaequipment.ca

Remote Operated Vehicles
www.deepocean.com
www.deepseaequipment.ca

Side Scan Sonar Systems
www.l-3klein.com
www.deepseaequipment.ca

Underwater Metal Detectors

www.consumer.minelab.com
www.aquascan.co.uk.products
www.garrett.com

Underwater Camera and Video Equipment

www.amphibico.com

Zodiac Boats Yamaha Engines

www.seamasters.net

Bibliography and References

Books

Brown, Richard. *History of Cape Breton Island.* London, U.K. 1869. Belleville, Ontario: Mika Publishing, 1979.

Dow, David Stuart. *The Cliffhanger House.* Antigonish, Nova Scotia: Formac Publishing Company, 1978.

Downey, Fairfax. *Louisbourg: Key to a Continent.* Englewood Cliffs, New Jersey: Prentice Hall, 1965.

Gosset, W.P. *The Lost Ships of the Royal Navy 1793-1900.* London, U.K.: Mansell, 1986.

Graham, Gerald S. *The Walker Expedition to Quebec 1711.* Toronto: The Champlain Society, 1953.

Gwyn, Julian. *The Enterprising Admiral The Personal Fortune of Admiral Peter Warren.* Montreal: McGill-Queen's Press, 1974.

Hichens, Walter W. *Island Trek.* Hantsport, Nova Scotia: Lancelot Press, 1982.

Hocking, Charles. *Dictionary of Disasters at Sea During the Age of Steam 1824-1962.* London: Lloyd's Register, 1969.

Horwood, Harold and Ed Butts. *Pirates and Outlaws of Canada 1610-1932*. Toronto, Canada: Doubleday Canada, 1984.

Lockery, Dr. Andrew. *Marine Archaeology and the Diver*. Toronto Canada: Atlantis Publishing, 1985.

Lyon, David. *The Sailing Navy List All the Ships of the Royal Navy Built, Purchased and Captured 1688-1860*. Chrysalis Books, Conway Maritime 1993.

Macdonald, S.D. *Ships of War Lost on the Coast of Nova Scotia and Sable Island, During the Eighteenth Century*. March 6, 1884.

MacMechan, Archibald. *There Go The Ships*. Toronto: McClelland & Stewart, 1928.

Mahan, Alfred Thayer. *The Influence of Sea Power upon History 1660-1805*. London, England: Bison Books, 1980.

Marsters, Roger. *Shipwreck Treasures – Disaster and Discovery on Canada's East Coast*. Halifax, Nova Scotia: Formac Publishing, 2002

McLennan, J.S. *Louisbourg From its Foundation to its Fall 1713-1758*. London: MacMillan & Co., 1918, second printing in 1969, third printing in 1983.

National Historic Sites, Environment Canada. *The Wreck of the Auguste*. Ottawa, 1992.

Olin, Philip. *Treasure The Business and Technology*. Micanopy, Florida: Key Lime Publishing Inc. 1991. Rev. ed. 1998.

Parkman, Francis. *Montcalm and Wolfe: The French and Indian War* first published in Boston in 1884. Republished by the Modern Library as *Montcalm and Wolfe: The Riveting Story of the Heroes of the French and Indian War*.

Patterson, George G. *Patterson's History of Victoria County*. First published in 1885. Reprinted by University College of Cape Breton Press, 1978, edited by W. James MacDonald.

Perry, Zella. *Sheep Shearing and Ship Wrecks, Seal Island*. Wallace, Nova Scotia. Published by the author, 1998.

Potter, John S. Jr. *The Treasure Divers Guide*. New York: Bonanza Books, 1972.

Rawlyk, George A. *Yankees at Louisbourg: The Story of the First Siege 1745*. Wreck Cove, Nova Scotia: Breton Books, 1999.

Readers Digest Association of Canada Ltd. *Heritage of Canada*. Ottawa: Readers Digest Association of Canada Ltd. 1978.

Rieseberg, Lt. Harry E. and A.A. Mikalow. *Fell's Guide to Sunken Treasure Ships of the World*. New York: Federick Fell, 1965.

Rigby, Carle A. *St. Paul Island: The Graveyard of the Gulf.* 1979, second printing in 2000.

Storm, Alex. *Canada's Treasure Hunt*. Winnipeg, Manitoba: Greywood Publishing Ltd. 1967.

Storm, Alex. *Seaweed and Gold*. Self-published, 2002

Trupp, Philip. *Tracking Treasure: Romance and Fortune Beneath the Sea and How to Find It*. Atlanta, Georgia: Acropolis Books, 1986.

Zinck, Jack. *Shipwrecks of Nova Scotia Volume 1*. Hantsport, Nova Scotia: Lancelot Press, 1975.

Zinck, Jack. *Shipwrecks of Nova Scotia Volume 2*. Hantsport, Nova Scotia: Lancelot Press, 1977.

Miscellaneous Sources

Brown, Richard and Glen T. Wright. *In Search of Shipwrecks: Government Archives Sources Relating to Marine Casualties in Canada*. Ottawa: Government Archives Division, National Archives of Canada, 1989. (Originally appeared in *FreshWater* v. 4 1989 pp. 14-20. (www.marmus.ca/marmus/wrecks.html)

Campbell, John. *The Campbell Journals*. Fourteen volumes covering day to day life on St. Paul Island from 1843 to 1921. Nova Scotia Archives and Records Management.

Campbell, Judith Veronica. *The History of Cape Breton Island.* 1975.

Canada Shipping Act. http://laws.justice.gc.ca/en/S-9/

Cape Breton's Magazine, Ron Caplan, Editor (Various Volumes). Wreck Cove, Cape Breton, Nova Scotia.

Christies Auction House. *Coins from the Feversham.* New York: Christies Auction House, catalogue, 1989.

Erskine, J. S. *St. Paul Island.* Journal of Education, Halifax, N.S. June 1955, pp 18-28, Nova Scotia Archives and Records Management.

Huntley, Frank H. *The Diary of Frank H. Huntley.* St. Paul Island, January 1, 1916 to June 30, 1920. Nova Scotia Archives and Records Management.

Little, Commander C.H. (ret'd). *Dispatches of Rear Admiral Sir Charles Hardy 1757-1758 and Vice Admiral Francis Holburne 1757.* Halifax: Occasional Paper # 2 of the Maritime Museum of Canada, June 1958.

MacKinnon, Robert. *The DEVCO Dive Scatarie Project.* Sydney, Nova Scotia: Cape Breton Development Corproation, 1974.

Nova Scotia Lighthouse Preservation Society Halifax, N.S. www.nslps.com

Ringer, Jim. *The Parks Canada Underwater Archaeological Excavation of the Auguste Site, Dingwall, Nova Scotia, 1977-78.* 1979.

Rose, Archie. *Wrecks of Halifax Harbour and Approaches.* Wreck chart, 1978.

Storm, Alex. *Shipwrecks of St. Paul Island.* Wreck chart, 1987.

St. Paul Island Historical Society, Kelly Fitzgerald, Dingwall, Cape Breton, Nova Scotia.

Treasure Trove Act. Nova Scotia Statutes www.gov.ns.ca/legi/legc/statutes/treasure.htm

Special Places Protection Act. Nova Scotia Statutes
www.gov.ns.ca/legi/legc/statutes/specplac.htm

Personal Interviews and Correspondence

Bob Anthony, former treasure hunter, professional diver and wreck diver who was part of the original team that discovered the *Auguste* in 1977 and was also part of the commercial archaeological salvage operation.

Ed Barrington, a professional salvage diver and wreck diver who was part of the original group that discovered the *Auguste* in 1977 and was also part of the commercial archaeological salvage operation.

David Barron, Northern Maritime Research, Author of the Atlantic Diver Guides and the Northern Shipwrecks Database CD Rom. Wreck diver and professional shipwreck researcher.

David Dow, historian and engineer involved with *DEVCO* and the *Dive Scatarie Project* in 1973.

Gerry Langille, former Royal Canadian Navy clearance diver and commercial diver who was part of the original team that discovered *Auguste* in 1977 and was also part of the commercial archaeological salvage operation.

Robert Marx, author, maritime historian and underwater archaeologist

Jimmy Mullins, fisherman, former treasure hunter, and wreck diver who was part of the original team that discovered the *Auguste* in 1977 and was also part of the commercial archaeological salvage operation.

John Oldham, former wreck diver, equipment manager and technician with the Parks Canada Underwater Marine Archaeology Unit in Ottawa.

Archie Rose, former Royal Canadian Navy clearance diver, professional salvage diver and wreck diver.

John Schumacher, treasure hunter, professional diver and wreck diver who was part of the team that discovered the *Auguste* in 1977 and was also part of the original commercial archaeological salvage operation.

Alex Storm, retired historian, treasure hunter and wreck diver who discovered the *Le Chameau* in 1966 and HMS *Feversham* and HMS *Leonidas* in 1968.

Terry Dwyer, author, underwater explorer and entrepreneur.

About the Author

Terry Dwyer was born in the coastal community of New Waterford, Cape Breton Island, Nova Scotia. He learned to scuba dive at the age of fifteen. Clearing propellors of rope and nets for local fishermen enabled him to start his first dive company, Sea Divers, at age sixteen. He spent five years working for a treasure hunting company and then spent the next twenty years of his life working in the Canadian scuba diving industry.

In 1992 he received a Rescue Commendation for an Act of Personal Bravery. In 1994 he founded the Nova Scotia Scuba Association. In 1995 his diving company Deep Star was selected by Lightstorm Entertainment (James Cameron) to provide the Diving Support Services for the motion picture *Titanic*, parts of which were filmed in Nova Scotia. In 1997, in recognition of outstanding contributions to the principals of the sport of scuba diving in Nova Scotia, he was awarded The Sports Network (TSN) Spirit of the Sport Award. He has authored and published numerous articles on scuba tourism, shipwrecks and shipwreck diving in Nova Scotia, and he is one of the foremost authorities on St. Paul Island. He is also a professional underwater videographer and photographer. In August 2000 he and Mark Stanton of *Divers Down Television* co-produced the Nova Scotia Tourism video, *Dive Nova Scotia*.

Terry has also served as an occupational diving operations and diving equipment consultant for the RCMP, various police forces, fire departments, and many other federal and provincial organizations and agencies. He has been working in the recreational, commercial and scientific diving industry for the past twenty years. In October 2005 he was elected as a "Fellow International" member to the prestigious Explorers Club. The Explorers club was founded in 1904 by a group of the worlds leading explorers. The Explorers Club is a multidisciplinary not-for-profit professional society dedicated to the advancement of field research, scientific exploration and the ideal that it is vital to preserve the instinct to explore.

Today he and his wife, Suzie operate Wreck Hunter Incorporated, a Halifax based shipwreck exploration and consulting company and Diver Down Industries, a scuba tourism and scuba retail business consulting company. They still organize private dive charters, expeditions and shipwreck search projects through Nova Scotia and Newfoundland.

Suzie and Terry Dwyer on the L'Auguste Project in 2006 in Aspy Bay, Cape Breton.